The Angler in the Shadows

Beware, Not all Doorways through which We Pass in Life are Two Way Portals, Choose Wisely!

BY BOB CIAMPITTI

DORRANCE
PUBLISHING CO
EST. 1920
PITTSBURGH, PENNSYLVANIA 15238

Dorrance Publishing Co
585 Alpha Drive
Pittsburgh, PA 15238
Visit our website at *www.dorrancebookstore.com*

ISBN: 978-1-6491-3843-9
eISBN: 978-1-6491-3861-3

The Angler
in the Shadows

BASED ON THE LIFE AND TIMES

AN AUTOBIOGRAPHICAL ACCOUNT
FROM INNOCENT CHILDHOOD
TO THE DAYS OF RETROSPECTION

A JOURNEY THROUGH
SPIRITUALITY
THE UNDERWORLD, SECRET SOCIETIES,
AND COUNCIL TO THOUSANDS

BASED ON ACTUAL CHARACTERS AND SITUATIONS
THE NAMES OF WHICH HAVE BEEN CHANGED TO PROTECT
THE PRIVACY OF THOSE NOT DIRECTLY CONNECTED
WITH THIS BOOK

ACKNOWLEDGMENT

I began this journey nine years ago in 2011. It is now 2020. The hiatus being fueled by a combination of considerations articulated by family and friends, being careful not to indict innocent players in my life.

Some of the content is sensitive and personal, as well as dangerous due to the cast of characters who may or will be referenced as the following chapters unfold.

The most cautious input came from my father, who after reading my first foray featured in a chapter written for a close friend who was publishing a faith-based book, my contribution was published as "THE CONTRACTOR."

My dad's input was to write with caution as some of the characters may still be alive and not featured in a flattering manner. Advice which I have taken seriously.

The second more encouraging and constant input came from my wife, who helped edit the context, which at times was hard for her to read, mostly because what she was reading was news to her and being digested for the first time.

My dad has since passed, but his words of caution ring clear in my ears, but my desire to finish what I started and return to writing this book before the memory of the experiences fades from memory never to be shared with others who might benefit from the story being told.

With all the above being weighed and considered, I have decided to complete the journey.

FOREWORD

The purpose of undertaking this journey was to give insight to the innocent and somewhat naïve youth of the lure and pending dangers that, for the most part, are imperceptible at first to the unsavory temptations thrown in the path of the unsuspecting novice who may be drawn to the lure of money, power, and influence.

There have been many books, movies, and television specials detailing and sometimes glamorizing the lives of those outside the realm of the honest and legal boundaries adhered to by the majority of a hard-working law-abiding society.

Little or no attention has been shown or articulated on the how and why the farm team for players necessary for an underworld society to grow and thrive in the years following the end of World War II were recruited. I was one of the players drawn to the dugout bench for just such a team yet to take the field.

This is my story as the events took place over a period of fifty years. Each chapter is a snippet at various stages of my life from childhood to adulthood. How it began and the direction it took.

THE ANGLER IN THE SHADOWS:

There comes a time in everyone's life when we must face the actuality of our existence.

A time when a balancing of actions over accomplishments must be weighed without the benefit of rationalization or veil of justification but rather the hard look of raw and sometimes decaying meat and fiber thrown into the brewing cauldron of ingredients we now call the essence of the life we have lived thus far.

For me, at the age of seventy-one, that time has come thrice, and each time I have come to a different conclusion of where I have been and where I am going.

In all honesty, I and the reader will not know what conclusion I have come to this time until the end of my chapters. For even now I am not sure where this writing will lead, how much I will have the stomach to recall or desire to reveal, but I make this promise at the outset... I will be as candid as humanly possible yet maintain the corpus of my existence and ability to live with one's self.

I have for years kept a journal of my life's events, both positive and negative, good and evil, successes and failures. I look back on those crude scrolls of my life with a longing hope that I can learn from them, grow, and correct, if possible, the wrongs I have done to others and more so to myself.

I have struggled to achieve the ability to live with myself through several methods of manipulation, selective memory, and the primal undeniable will to survive being the top two.

My reply to those who inquire into my personal life, which I admit are repulsive in nature yet require a response, lest I not be left in peace, is:

> *I am not proud of everything I have done in life, but I regret nothing. I did what had to be done to prevent others from doing to me what I was about to do to them. They may not like or respect me, but they will fear me. We are all playing this game we call life, and the fact that I have achieved a better understanding of how the game works and how to win does not make me an evil person but merely someone who possesses the ability to see a check coming and quickly negate it with a check mate."*

One might ask then, why would I choose this time and place to reveal to others, some of whom are still playing the game and some who I still come in contact with as opponents in this game, my close to the vest tactics and strategies on how to weigh, measure, and dispose of anyone who enters the arena of power, influence, and material gain where I am a combatant?

I look upon the strengths and weaknesses of others and quickly determine how best to dilute, undermine, and destroy those elements of their character and personality that might work to their advantage in the coming battle. I look not at the person or his human components, considering them to be neither attributes nor flaws but merely targets on a playing field to neutralize.

I gave fair warning. *There is no depth to which I will not sink to win. These are not cufflinks; they are curb feelers!*

I Am The Contractor

I cannot explain how I arrived at this place without giving the reader some insight into where and how my life began, both the physical and spiritual aspects. I will need to recall for myself and reveal to the reader the mileposts along the way that gave rise to my strong ties with the Catholic faith, questioning that faith, losing it, and regaining it several times along the way and finally, at this stage of my life, returning once again to the place of beginning. This time with a stronger conviction of who I want to be, where that strength comes from, and how I have regained the inner peace and serenity not found in worldly accomplishments but rather through spiritual gains.

CONTENT

CHAPTER ONE
The Early Years, Searching For Direction

I was the middle child of a second-generation Italian-American heritage whose father came from an average, work through the depression family and whose grandfather kept a small candy store in South Philadelphia. My father, after returning from the military of World War II, attended night school and worked during the day toward his eventual career as a real estate broker. It seemed he was either showing houses or attending classes in the evening. I don't recall much about interacting with him in those early years, but I do, however, remember him being there for the important things, like holidays, family gatherings, and evening meals, as well as for any illnesses, which caused me to remain home from school.

My mother was one of seven children of working-class Italians who grew out of a strong sense of family, having grown up in a small three-room house just off the Italian Market in South Philadelphia. I had numerous Compares and Comares (Godfathers and Godmothers), a title of honor in Italian families; with them came the lessons of years of experience in how to get along with others, survive, and prosper.

But I was a restless child and frustrated at the prospect of having to live in my own skin, the skin of a child who felt no one took seriously. I couldn't wait to grow up and show the world what I was capable of; for me life moved too damn slow. While other kids were out playing with friends laughing and taking life as it came, I was sitting in a room that I shared with my older brother, thinking of ways to make a few bucks with hopes that in doing so, I could gain some respect and with that freedom, freedom from what twenty-five cents a week allowance for chores performed could possibly produce.

At the age of seven, while still in second grade and in a public school, I came up with my first enterprise. Running errands for neighbors who were stuck at home raising children and maintaining a household for husband and family. This was a start, but it lacked growth as I could only work within a three city-block area, but it was a start, but in my mind, it was small time and without a sense of adventure... I NEED SOMETHING ELSE, SOMIETHIHNG NOT YET THOUGHT OF!

WE ARE IN SOUTH PHILADELPHIA IN A SMALL ROW HOME ON A TYPICAL CITY STREET.

The sun is just beginning to rise on a cold, fall Saturday morning. Everyone else in the house is asleep. My older brother still buried under the covers of his twin bed on the other side of our small room.

I instinctively rush to the rear window, opening it I pull on the clothes line, which is connected to a pulley attached to a pole in the rear yard and back to the window of my friend Butch's bedroom in the house next door. There is a small metal lifesaver box attached with a string hanging from the line that we use to send messages to each other without our parents knowing what we are planning.

Today the note reads, "Meet me in the back yard after breakfast."

Wow! What great adventure was Butch planning for today? He was an only child of a tailor and a very permissive mother who doted on him constantly. He was allowed to do almost anything, which puts us in some interesting yet dangerous situations.

After breakfast, we meet up as planned. My hopes for an adventure are dashed. He tells me he's going to visit his grandparents on their upstate farm. He wanted to stay home and play with me, but his folks said no. I guess for a pair of seven-year-old kids, that was asking the impossible. Funny thing though, I never thought of myself as a child. I thought of myself as an adventurer waiting for something spectacular to happen just around the corner, maybe today would be that day.

I took a deep breath and went back inside where my mother was preparing a bowl of Sugar Pops Cereal with slices of banana, my favorite breakfast for a Saturday morning. I finished my bowl in a matter of minutes as my mom asked why I was in such a hurry, it was only 7 A.M. and my brother and dad had not even showed up at the table yet. I gave her a kiss and said I was on my way to an adventure.

My mom just smiled and said, "Okay, Big Bob, be careful."

And so my life's adventure begins, not with an obvious bang or fireworks but with a step out my front door. I grabbed my woolen coat and hat off the hook on the cellar way landing, stepped over my brother who was fixated on the latest episode of *Flash Gordon* and yelling back to my mom, I'm going out to play, I put my hand on the inside door knob, took a deep breath, and stepped out into what could be the day that changed my life.

My eyes grew wide open as I gazed at the surroundings looking for a neighborhood friend or anyone with whom I could engage in planning a day of fun. My head was turning quickly right and left searching for movement....nothing, not even a dog or cat, nothing. I took an involuntary deep breath, lowered my chin on my chest and was about to go back inside when out of the corner of my eye, I spotted movement. Around the corner came a figure, a tall man well-dressed wearing a grey topcoat and a hat to match, the brim of the hat was turned down covering most of his face. He was walking in my direction, and I just froze there. I never saw him before, and he didn't look like any of the blue-collar working-class men I knew from the neighborhood; my mind raced as he approached where I was standing on the top step of my row home.

Now in those days, every neighborhood had a corner store of one kind or another, and our street was no different. On one corner, there was a grocery store and a shoe maker shop, at the other end of our street there was a pool hall. We never walked that way unless it was absolutely unavoidable, and if we did, we were to cross over to the other side of the street, look down or straight ahead, and walk as quickly as our little feet could take us.

The year was 1955, and my parents would have been more proud finding me sitting in the front row of the Trockadero Burlesque Club than finding me near the pool hall. I was a seven-year-old Italian Catholic boy, and even at that age I had been lectured on numerous occasions by both my parents and grandparents about keeping a safe distance from the wise guy underworld figures that hung out and ran those types of establishments.

Yet there I was, eyes fixated on this figure talking to himself in an agitated manner now directly in front of my house.

He stops, turns toward me, and as he lifts his head to speak, his dark eyes lock on mine, and in a broken English dialect, asks if know what time the shoe maker shop opens.

Without waiting for an answer, he inquires further, "They shine shoes there, too, don't they?"

I reply in like manner, "Ten o'clock, and yes, they do."

Lowering his eyes, he whispers, "That's too late," then looking up once again, asks, "Can you shine shoes?"

My shoulders perked up, my mouth begins to move, and without thinking, I reply, "Hell yeah!" I learned by watching the old black man in front of the bar on Porter Street, then I whispered to myself, "Where the hell did that come from? He must have heard me."

Shaking his head and with a crooked smile, he smirks, "Great, kid, go get your shoe shine box and meet me at the corner." Holy crap! The corner, oh no ,I thought, that is the pool hall, what am I going to do now? Crap, I thought, think fast, this is an opportunity to see what goes on inside and make some money for myself... I got it, I'll tell my mom I am going to knock on doors and see if anyone wanted me to shine shoes. Now my mom didn't mind so much as long as I stayed in the neighborhood and was home in time for supper. My dad, however, would never approve; he had to shine

4

shoes at his father's candy store during the depression and he swore no son of his would ever have to stoop to that level again. I, on the other hand, had no pride when it came to making money. It was the ticket to freedom and a way to gain respect from those older than me and make them listen to what I had to say. I hated being thought of as a child who was to be seen and not heard. I wanted to grow up fast and making money, I thought, was a way to get there.

As he turns and walks away, I open the door behind me, run back inside, again stepping over my brother who now has his *Flash Gordon* Decoder Ring in one hand and punching my leg with the other, shouting my plan to my mother as I rush past her to the basement, grab my shoe shine box, kiss her good bye.

"I'll be home before dinner," I shout. Having to once again cross in front of my brother and *Flash Gordon,* I hit the off button, shutting the TV in retaliation for the earlier punches, and out the door I flew, leaping from the top step to the sidewalk and down the street to the pool hall on the corner. It wasn't Oz, I thought, but it was close.

In my excitement, I forgot what my parents had warned me about and who I might be dealing with once I crossed that imaginary line, a line they told me had only one direction, and if crossed, you could never return.

I banged as hard as I could on the side door. From within I hear a faint, "What the hell," then the squeak of the peephole as it slides open. "What!" came a cry from inside. Now remember, I am a seven-year-old four-foot-tall, blond hair, blue eyed, slender build Italian boy. "What?" came another cry, "I can't see you."

"Oh! Sorry," I said, "I'm the shoe shine boy."

"Hold on," came a reply, and the peep hole closed. In what seemed like an eternity, I stood, waiting, hoping no one in the neighborhood saw me near the pool hall. The door opens and there stands the man I met just a short time earlier. "Come on in, what's your name?" he asks.

"Bobby," I reply, "but my friends call me Big Bob."

"Big Bob," he repeats, "well, I am Jimmy and I run this joint." With his hand on my shoulder, he yells out to about twenty other guys there playing pool and drinking espresso coffee, "Guys, this is Big Bob, he is our new in-house shoe shine boy, take care of him," he shouts. "Now how about my shoes? I have an important meeting and I want them to look sharp, can you do that?"

"No problem," I reply, "just sit down and I will have them looking new in about fifteen minutes."

Time passes, "Great job, Big Bob, how much do I owe you?"

"Well, if I am the in-house shoe shine boy and you are the boss here, then the first shine is on the house."

He laughs. "I like you, kid," he says, then yells, "This kid does a great shoe shine," and one by one, I meet every guy in the joint and make about ten dollars in a few hours. That's a lot of money in 1955 for a seven-year-old kid, hell, that's a lot of money for anyone to make in a few hours. As I am getting ready to leave, Jimmy returns and says, "Nice meeting you, Big Bob. How about you come around a couple times a week after school and on weekends, you could do well here," he says.

"Great, I will," he shakes my hand and lets me out the side door.

I pause for a minute and think, how dumb does that sound, Big Bob... Big Bob, why nobody calls me that, it's a fictional character in my dreams that my mom tells me she hears me saying in my sleep. It's my idea of myself when I am older and a street hero, it's cool in my sleep but sounds really lame when you say it out loud. Next time I see Jimmy, I'll ask him and the other guys to just call me Bobby.

I must have been walking in a semi-trance, not noticing my neighborhood friends walking along side of me asking, "Where you been? We were looking for you to play football."

"Football," I screeched, "I don't have time for games. I am in business now," showing them how much money I just made. Everyone just stopped, jaws open, eyes glazed in total silence.

Then my best friend Alfred asked, "Where did you get all that money?"

"Shining shoes," I said.

"Shining shoes, that's only a dime, how many shoes did you shine?" he asked.

"I'm not sure, about twenty. I am the in-house shoe shine boy at the pool hall now," I retorted, again dead silence.

"Are you out of your freaking mind?" came several voices, "you're not allowed in there, hell, no one is allowed in there."

"Yeah," I snapped back, "well, I am and you guys better not tell anyone either."

Then it came to me, why would they keep quiet? I wouldn't keep quiet either, he's making all this money, I'd think, and I'm not. Say something quick, I told myself before they go home and figure this out. "GUYS," I said softly, "listen, we can have our own thing going here if we stick together." I can tell they are listening, waiting, what's next? "You all know we are not allowed near that place, right? Well, paper boys and shoe shine boys are looked at differently by the police, and if you guys cover for me with our parents and neighbors, I'll pay each of you twenty-five cents a week." There were only six of them, I thought, that was a small price to pay for the cover, I continued, "But if you guys help me get customers, I'll pay you even more."

They looked at each other and then at me and said, "Okay, we're in."

"Let's swear on it," I said; each of us put one hand in the center and we swore to keep the secret.

1949 with my parents and brother Bill left

1954 In front of Fells School 1st grade

Blond Hair Blue Eyed Italian Boy, sitting on a Getaway Horse!
Must have been an omen of things to come, it was only a short ride to the pool
hall at the end of my street

9

Brother Bill & friend Larry Looking North on Darien Street

1957 My mom looking for me to put on leather jacket (I was at the pool hall)

1958 Christmas on Darien Street My dad and grandfather

Easter, I am the smaller of the two bookends, at the age of eight years I am at the height of my street business. How could you say no to a shoe shine from a kid who looks this innocent?

1950 My grandfather Ciampitti in front of his candy store/ Poker Hall

1950 Close family friend with hidden agenda

CHAPTER TWO
Expanding My Sphere Of Infulence

Months go by, it's a snowy day, grey sky, not much activity outside, school is closed for the day. It's about 9 A.M., most of the men have left early to get to work, so no one is shoveling snow. It's too early to go to the pool hall. Now a light goes on in my head, so I run back inside and grab a note book from my school bag and a pencil. My first stop is at the door of my best friend Alfred; he is watching cartoons but opens the door in his pajamas.

"Get dressed, Al, I need your help." While he is getting dressed, I begin at one end of the street knocking on doors and asking if I could shovel their walk. I reason with them that with all this snow, their husbands would probably be late getting home and not in the mood to shovel "It will be your gift for them," I say. Most smile and ask how much. "Well," I reply, "if you give me a quarter now and a quarter when I finish, I will clear your walk now and again if needed when the snow stops, that's fair, don't you think?" I say.

"You're a real little businessman, Bobby," they tell me, "why yes, that is a fair price," and hand me the first quarter. What I was really doing was making sure no other kid came along and took my customer before I got back, kind of insurance against competition. Everything is working swell; by the time Alfred caught up with me, I had signed up twenty or so houses. I told him to get the rest of our gang, bring shovels, and meet me in front of the grocery store.

The snow has started to lighten up, and it is about noon when all six of the guys show up. I have deposits from almost the whole neighborhood now, that's about sixty houses and fifteen dollars in my pocket. If I wait another hour before they start shoveling, I probably will only have to clear the walks once. I tell my friends that I have all these houses to shovel and will give them a quarter for each one they clear, and while we are waiting for the snow to stop, I will treat them to lunch at Nat's Deli around the corner. Now a Coke and a grilled cheese sandwich is thirty-five cents, and for six guys, that's only $2.35 with a tip. I still get to keep $12.65. They get to keep the quarter from however many houses they shovel. It's a win-win. My friends are happy, and I am happy.

I pay Nate for the food in advance because it's almost time to get my shine box and go over to the pool hall.

"Do a nice job," I warn, "it's a long winter, and we want the repeat business."

"Okay, Bobby," they reply, "see you later," and I am out the door.

Grey sky, but the snow has stopped. *Great*, I thought, *they will only have to shovel once*. I am walking down my front steps, which I shoveled for free, it's my house and they feed me here. I have a smirk on my face.

I am wearing a black wool coat and a wool hat with ear flaps that tie around your chin, but I never tie it, looks too sissified, I am now too cool for such nonsense. I get to the side door of the pool hall and knock.

"It's Bobby," I yell and the door opens. It's about one o'clock and the place is packed. All the wise guys are indoors and their shoes are dirty from the snow.

"Hey, Bobby," I hear, "I need a good shine."

"Okay, give me a minute," I reply as I hang up my coat and hat and go over to the corner chair Jimmy set up for me months ago. It's my own spot and I feel important; these guys make me feel important. There are quite a few sailors coming here now. The Naval Base is not that far away, and they can drink and gamble in here without worrying about the MP'S. No one gets in here unless Jimmy lets them in.

Then while I am shining shoes, Jimmy comes over for a shine, and while I am buffing, he asks, "Bobby, do you know where the Porter House Bar is?"

Without looking up, I reply, "Sure, Jimmy, it's only a few blocks up from here. I pass it all the time when I go with my mom to the stores on 7th Street."

"Yeah," he says, "that's the place. How would you like to do a few shines there? My friend owns the joint," he continues, "he would love to hook you up there, it would be worth your while to get more customers."

"Sure," I said, finishing up his shine, "it's within the area I am allowed to travel from home, so it shouldn't be a problem."

"It's early," Jimmy says, "so let me know when you are finished here and I'll walk over with you and introduce you to my friend Pauley." As planned, after about an hour, Jimmy says, "Are you ready, Bobby?"

"Sure," I reply, and we walk down Porter Street to the bar and go inside. Pauley comes over to meet us.

Jimmy says, "Pauley, this is Bobby, he is our guy at the pool hall and he does great shines, maybe you can help him out."

"No problem," says Pauley, "can you work now, kid?" he asks.

"Sure," I reply. "I have about an hour and a half before dinner."

"Great." He gives Jimmy a wink and a pat on his shoulder and Jimmy leaves. Pauley shows me around and tells everyone who I am and to get their shoe shines from me from now on. Everyone smiles, and one by one, I ply my trade.

It's getting close to dinner time, and I tell Pauley I have to leave; he thanks me and asks when I can come back, but without waiting for an answer he continues, "Well, work that out with Jimmy. Nice meeting you, Bobby."

"Nice meeting you, too," I say, "and thanks for the work."

I grab my hat and coat and I'm out the door. I have a pocket full of money and I keep one hand in that pocket for protection and my shine box in the other. I am walking at a fast pace because I want to stop at the pool hall before going home. Jimmy always told me, never count your money in public and never let people know how much you have. If I get there in time, I can count it, wrap it in one of the slap rags in my shoe box, and head home to hide it. Jimmy is still there and asked how I did.

"Great," I said, "thanks, Jimmy."

"No problem, kid," he said. After a short pause, he asks if I will be back on Saturday and if I could show up around noon. He said he had an idea of how I could make a little more money if I was interested.

"Are you kidding?" I said. Next to my mom's meals, making money was my favorite thing to do.

"Okay, Bobby, see you then." As he walks away, he looks back and says, "Remember, watch your money."

"I know, Jimmy, thanks." I go to the bar and trade my change for bills; wrapping them in a rag, I tuck it down under the paste cans and leave for home. It's only a short walk up the street.

This was a start, but it lacked growth as I could only work within a three-city block area, but it was a start! I began to expand, painting street addresses at the curb for all the row homes existing within my realm, then things took off. Painting iron railings, yard fences, and gates to returning trash cans to a neighbor's yard after each trash pickup, in winter I added shoveling snow to clearing off cars and cutting access ways for working men to get out of plowed in parking spaces in order to get to work. These had to be done either in the evenings after dinner or before school started.

In order to protect my income environment, I made deals with homeowners to perform these tasks in advance, collecting a small deposit, which would prevent them from giving the job to another kid who saw what I was doing and tried to cash in on the idea.

Now that I had the work, I needed help. I recruited my neighborhood friends to work for a fair wage and that kept competition to a minimum. If someone did give the work to another kid, I would have one of the local bully's track them down and convince them to stay out of my turf. Of course this also required a small fee, which I was happy to pay to keep the peace. This may sound a little odd for a seven-year-old boy, but it is how my journey began.

By now I was eight-years-old and in third grade. It was a wonderful time in my life. A local new Catholic Parish had just been completed, a new elementary school opened along with it and I wanted to go. My best friend Alfred was already enrolled and would start third grade there that September. I wanted more than anything to go and after telling my parents how important it was to me; they agreed to enroll both my brother and I for the fall semester.

2020 The Old Neighborhood The Way It Looks Today

2020 The Old Neighborhood The Way It Looks Today

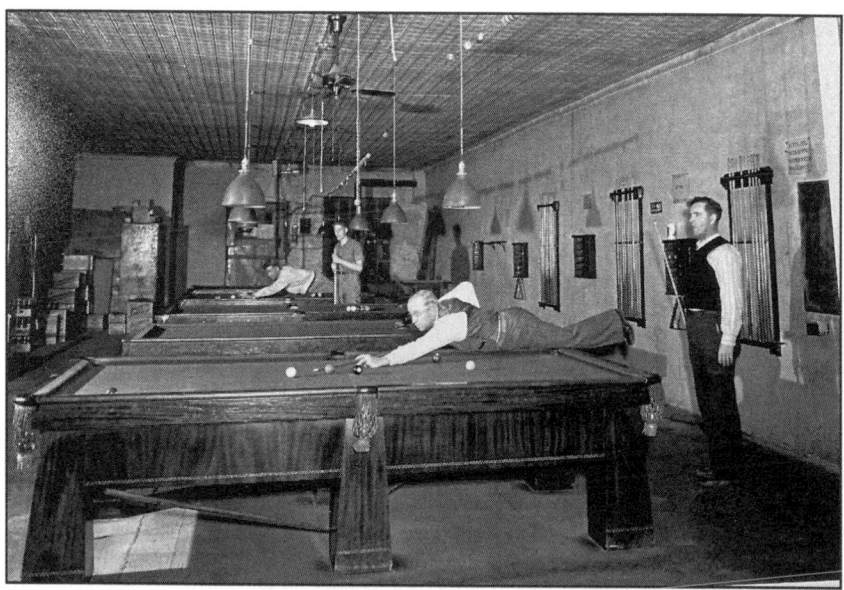

Life at the pool hall 1950's typical pool hall interior at the time

1950's Typical shoe shine boy after a long day, counting his money

1958 My spot in the pool hall set up for me by Jimmy

2020, Pool Hall Main Entrance off Porter Street

Jimmy's private entrance off Darien Street

1960 Easter on Darien street. Cousin Tony approaching me with Silver Dollars, an Italian custom at that time, they were to save, not spend. I still have all those coins!

1960 Easter on Darien Street, my friend Harry, looking North, cousin Tony in background

At the jersey Shore with brother Bill and friend Larry

CHAPTER THREE
Spiritual Connection And Rejection

I am in third grade now in a new Catholic School that just opened in our area and I am drawn to my newfound faith. I have a love for Jesus and want to be just like him, I wanted to be a priest

(I must admit that even now as I recall that, "Somewhere in time," my eyes are full, this is something I have not thought about for a long time). Suppressed feelings remembered!

As I recall, I gathered all my friends, business associates, and relayed my new idea. We had a base of operation and a list of steady clients, all of whom had children or varying ages who we could recruit for a new...wait for it!

Children's Church. I went about collecting the items needed to set up a church in my parents' basement, I would put on my black Sunday suit, black shirt with white collar, along with a black felt hat. I had rosary beads on my belt and my Sunday Missal in hand, and along with my new found apostles, went door to door talking about Jesus Christ, asking if I could bless their house with a bottle of holy water I "borrowed" from the fountain at the church after which I would politely ask for a small donation, which would go toward expanding our efforts and giving some of it to the school for the Catholic Charites Appeal. We also purchased a few "Pagan Babies," a practice well-known to my age group who went to Catholic School.

After weeks of close study and attention to the mass at church, I was able to begin holding mass in my parent's basement every

Saturday evening at 6:00 P.M. I used grape juice for wine and white only NECO Wafers for Communion. Of course there was the passing of a wicker basket for offerings. Even some of the adult neighbors came to watch as their children behaved in a fashion equal to that expected of them at Sunday Mass. No one was laughing at me now, they were amazed. My parents, especially my father, was a little concerned. My dad told me later on in life that at the time he feared I had little concept of childhood, and seeing that I had the ability to influence others without regard or knowledge of how to handle such a responsibility, that gave him cause for worry. He knew a responsibility like that came with consequences. He also knew that character trait was usually learned later on in life and not at eight years of age. He feared I was beginning to believe I was able to follow my own will, and worse, believed I could accomplish the desired results. He attempted to slowly apply additional controls on my activities to keep me from the harm he felt would inevitably come. I did not heed the warning and became consumed in my own ability.

I ran my life at that young age by a simple code. *"Rather than follow in the footsteps of those who have gone before you, cut a new path and leave a trail."* I thought I was on the right path, but I was becoming something else. I can't to this day tell you what it was, but there was a force at work, unseen, quiet, yet purposeful, driving me in a direction of which I had no knowledge or control. Could this have been the work of someone or something with motives far different than what I thought, something more sinister? Good is easy to spot, but evil comes in many forms, some are obvious and some are cloaked in flowers and perfume.

Either way at eight years of age, these concepts were far too complex for a young mind to behold, especially the mind of a boy who thought he had it all figured out.

Fourth grade, nine years of age and already feeling the weight of responsibility, the friends and acquaintances I made in life so far are depending on me for the next move. They were excited at their ability to do and accomplish things no other children we knew were doing at that time. We had a following of kids, both younger and older; it was great fun, but it was now work.

I sat in class that first day in September waiting to see who my nun or lay teacher would be that year. I couldn't help but think of how I could use what I had learned to help other kids. I was lucky, I had loving parents and a large immediate family of grandparents, aunts, uncles, cousins, and caring neighbors.

Then it happened, my day dreaming about happiness and the good in the world was shattered; my life was about to take a sharp turn. The classroom door opened and slammed shut only to reveal a tall, skinny sour puss St. Joseph's nun with arms neatly concealed in the sleeves of her habit, those sleeves also concealing a heavy wooden ruler. I would later come to find that ruler was not for measuring but for cracking against the knuckles of any child not in compliance with the rules of this Nazi trained enforcer. I will not mention her name here, for the wretch may still be alive. Maybe retired by now and working at a slaughter house for harmless animals in the Midwest.

Nonetheless there she stood saying nothing but taking mental inventory of the sixty some students sitting before her, their hands and arms folded, shaking in their seats waiting for the venom to spew from her lifeless white lips. It seemed like an eternity before she spoke. Then finally she wrote her God forsaken name on the blackboard with a large piece of white chalk that screeched along as if it were an omen of bad things to come. And they did.

She was the worst kind of Catholic that could exist in the mind of a nine-year-old Italian boy. A pale white Irish Catholic nun with an open dislike for Italians. This would later support my belief that God does have a sense of humor. Why else would he send this creature to a new parish consisting of a population of about 98% Italians. It occurred to me that maybe God didn't much care for her either. She was what my mother later would refer to as a frustrated virgin! My mother was usually dead on when it came to judging people's character.

It didn't take long before she would isolate several of the boys in the class to torture on a regular basis while the few Margaret

Marys of the world found favor in her Hansel and Gretel world. By mid-October of that year, it came down to two sorry souls, Anthony and I.

Every day the mental barrage of derogatory comments would begin only to find us both being put into the coat closet, having to occasionally endure the door opening to reveal this cursed woman sprinkling us with Holy Water, claiming we were possessed by the devil.

> *Tears now forming in my eyes as I recall those days...so sad...but that bitch made me stronger than ever and determined to get even, and whenever possible, to inflict as much harm and punishment upon her and my parish as I could.!*

When out of nowhere, an opportunity presented itself, my brother Bill told me the church was going to form a choir and they were having tryouts the following Saturday.

And so we went, several of the boys from the neighborhood, myself included. Most of us made the cut, but I was told I had a range in my voice that allowed me to sing high-soprano. I didn't know what that meant, but I was the only one in the group who could reach those notes.

Now I was special, and the parish pastor made sure we all got plenty of hours of practice, and on numerous occasions, he came to my classroom to get me himself. I was now untouchable by that SS Trooper who ran the classroom, but poor Anthony was not so lucky. I thought of him every day the rest of that year.

As for me, it was back to business as usual, screw the Children's Church idea, it seemed to me that those set in authority as representatives of the church had no idea what the Bible taught, and if God could allow children to be treated with such indifference and distain then, from here on out, God was on his own and I would take care of myself.

CHAPTER FOUR

Deeper Into The Murky Waters

It's a sunny Saturday morning.

The family has finished breakfast, and my dad is off to work, my mom is cleaning up the kitchen, and as usual, the latest episode of *Flash Gordon* is on TV.

I am dressed and ready to head down to the pool hall to see what Jimmy has in mind.

Aside from him, I have two male role models in my life, my dad and my Uncle Nick.

My dad is a soft-spoken man, dedicated to his family and working during the day while attending college in the evening in order to make a better life for us. Between building his real estate business and finishing school under the GI Bill, I have limited interaction with him at this stage of my life. I don't begrudge him because I know things are tough all over, and he is doing what needs to be done.

My uncle, on the other hand, is a mountain of a man with strong convictions of right and wrong. He is uncompromising, short tempered, and once provoked, never backs down. But he is a good man, gentle of spirit, and a true friend to everyone he knows. A man you could count on when in need, no matter what the danger or consequence to himself, he is there for you. He is the antithesis of my dad and my well-source of confidence and sometimes arrogance in my street persona. They are my family, not the kind you think of in an Italian neighborhood, that was Jimmy, but my biological family,

and I know they will always be on my side, but guys like Jimmy…
well, you never really know.

After a kiss goodbye from my mom and the usual interaction
with the number one fan club member of *Flash Gordon*, I am out the
door with my shine box heading for the pool hall.

"Hey, Bobby, how ya doin! Jimmy's in the back, go ahead in,"
says the bar keep. Jimmy is sitting at a table talking to Pauley from
the tavern on Porter Street.

"Sorry, Jimmy, I didn't know…"

He stops me short and says, "Come in, Pauley was just leaving."
Pauley says hello with a pat on my shoulder and walks out the door.
"I hear you been working the neighborhood pretty good lately with
your pals," he says.

"Yeah," I reply with a sense of pride, "I like working hard any
making my own way."

"What about that priest thing I heard about and your basement
church?" he asks.

"How do you know about that?" I reply.

"I know everything in the neighborhood," he says.

"Well, screw all that," I say, "why did you want to see me?"

"You have a lot of street smarts for a little kid, you have a lot of
potential."

Losing my smile. I snap back, "I may be little, but I am not just
a kid. I am somebody my friends count on…"

"Sorry, Bobby, no disrespect, you're right, we count on you, too; in
fact we have a proposition for you if you want to make more money."

THE NEXT WORDS OUT OF MY MOUTH WILL CHANGE
MY LIFE FOREVER!

"Sure, Jimmy, you can count on me, what do you want me to do?"

"Well, you are already working here and the Porter House, so
you only have to make a slight adjustment to your routine a couple
times a week and you're good to go."

Jimmy, now standing, walks over to me and hands me a few
slips of paper. "See these?" he whispers, "well, when *you* finish shining shoes here, I will give you papers like these; all you have to do

is hide them in your box, and when you go to see Pauley, just give them to him when nobody is watching."

"That's it?" I say.

"Well, no, there is one other thing. Do you know the hardware store on the corner of Mildred and Shunk Street?"

"Yeah," I reply.

"Well, there is a friend of ours on that corner named Harry, Harry the Horse. When you leave Pauley's, he will give you a few more papers and you just give them to Harry on your way home."

"Okay," I say, "but how does that make more money for me?" I question. Jimmy starts to laugh.

"Gotta love you, kid, you don't miss a trick, well..." Now he's leaning over to whisper in my ear, "Every time you make the rounds, each of us will give you a dollar, plus the dime for the shine, that's three dollars three times a week. One more thing, Bobby, I know you burn your wax tins before a shine, but don't do it near these papers; they'll evaporate," he says. Although I am confused, I make like I know what he is talking about. I just do as he says and move on.

"When do I start?"

"Right now, if you can." That was the answer I wanted to hear. "Let me know when you are ready to go and I will give you the papers." After about two hours, I finished at the hall and go find Jimmy. Over in my corner of the room, Jimmy hands me a roll of papers and tells me to put them at the bottom of the box for Pauley, hands me a buck and a pat on the back. And just like Jimmy said, I drop off and pick up at each location, make my money, no questions asked, and head home.

A few months go by, and things are working out just great, I am making a lot of money, and even though my parents are giving me twenty-five cents allowance each week for chores and stuff, I don't need it and help my mom and dad with things around the house, but they are getting suspicious on how I can buy things for myself on just my allowance. I have to be more careful and hide the money at the pool hall. I am smart enough to know I can't get away with this much longer. But that is another story.

1945 My Uncle Nick before I was born, he was a really big guy.
The boy next to him was 4 foot 3 inches tall.

1962 Christmas on Broad Street My 7-year-old brother, Bruce, in background

1963 June My elementary school prison

Graduation Day, my final escape from choir and the coat closet

CHAPTER FIVE
Living In Denial

It's now spring, and I have added a few other businesses to my list, like putting out and returning trash cans to neighbor's yards, painting the iron railings on their front steps, painting house addresses at the curb line, every house had to have one and there were literally hundreds of houses in the neighborhood, and painting the wooden rear yard fences.

My guys were busy all the time, and I was making a little cash off each one. While the gang was busy with the jobs I had lined up, I was still running numbers from the pool hall, to The Porter House, and finally to Harry.

One day I finally had the nerve to ask Harry what was it about those papers, why did they always smell like eggs, and why did they feel slippery.

Harry just looked at me and said, "Because this is Flash Paper."

With a shrug of my head, I inquired, "What's Flash Paper?"

"Watch," he said, and after reading what was on the slips and making notations in a little tablet he kept in his vest pocket, he opens his hand, put the slips of paper in his palm, and with a quick touch of the cigarette, he was smoking the papers evaporated in a puff of smoke, like a flash!

"What was that?" I asked.

"Well, kid, these thin pieces of tissue paper have a group of numbers on them from Pauley and they are rubbed with sulfur; if anyone comes too close, I just touch the paper with my cigarette and no more paper, get it, kid?"

"I get it."

I sure did get it; I was not just a kid doing small odd jobs in the area. I was running numbers for the wise guys in the neighborhood. I was a big shot with my friends because they all made money with me and nobody gave us any grief.

I began to block out the obvious; at ten years of age, I am living a double life, the one my biological family knows as a cute, blond hair, blue eyed boy with a bright smile and a friendly disposition and the kid my street family knows as Bobby, who keeps his promises and delivers on his word.

A kid who has earned the respect of the street powers that be and the protection that goes along with it.

My mother knew I was shining shoes but didn't know I was doing most of my shines at the pool hall. She saw no harm in my earning a few dollars, but that would not be the case had she known where I was, so I kept that a secret and it worked; as long as I was home before dinner, no questions were asked, so I never had to lie.

But running numbers for Wise Guys, that would devastate her for sure. But for me at the time, I couldn't believe my good fortune, what a hook up. Three times a week, I would perform this Flash Paper ritual, and three times a week, I would earn three dollars and thirty cents for the effort. This of course was on top of the money I made from other patrons of both the pool hall and the tap room. In all I would average about twenty-five dollars a week from the shoe shine business alone, but when added to all the other ventures I had going, I was grossing about forty dollars in a good week.

To put that into perspective, the year was 1957 and the average-working man was earning about sixty to seventy dollars net a week for forty hours labor. I became a staple at those establishments and very friendly with some of the Wise Guys, and they looked out for me as well. By the time I was ten and eleven, I was loaning money to guys playing pool, and the "Wise Guys" showed me how to maximize that venture by collecting twice the amount loaned by week's end. In the event someone didn't pay up, the boys would make sure they found the money needed and paid me. This seemed to me to be the way of the world and a good way to earn money. I also learned how to dispose of Flash Paper quickly should anyone I didn't know started asking questions.

This was my first exposure to the world my parents desperately tried to keep us away from, but it seemed harmless at the time, but they didn't know I was making that kind of money or that I even knew those type of people.

I am a twelve-year-old still running my game, but now I am loaning money to the sailors who hang out at the pool hall waiting for their payday. Jimmy knows who they are and makes sure I always get repaid, usually double the loan, on a weekly basis. Jimmy does it on a larger scale but lets me have some of the small stuff. I think it makes him feel good.

When I wasn't shining shoes, I was learning how to play pool; many of the guys would show me how to read the table, how to make a bank shot, and how to play the angles. Without they or I actually knowing it, they were teaching me geometry.

To keep the games interesting, they would put a quarter on the rail as a wager, and I would match the bet. I knew sometimes they would let me win by deliberately missing a shot. It taught me how to be competitive, and depending on the bet, it taught me how to spot a mismatch and skip the wager. They knew exactly what they were doing, and it was an education I would never have gotten in Catholic School.

Looking back on the early days when all I wanted to do was be like Jesus and even had thoughts of being a priest, I wonder, how did I get to this place? A place where nothing matters, except money, influence, and power.

RECAP:

It took a while to get here, but this is how my story begins, it is this background that will give clarity and basis for what takes place from now on.

By the time I reached the eighth grade, we had moved from our small neighborhood street to a large house on Broad Street with all new furniture and a new car in the driveway. My dad had always taught us to live below our means and always be humble and caring about others. If this was below our means, I thought, then we must be doing pretty well, but I still had not yet learned to appreciate my dad and his ways.

I never did have a great relationship with my father at that point in my life. He was a kind, soft spoken, gentle man who always found that compromise was a better solution than confrontation. I didn't agree and thought him to be somewhat of a push over. I had grossly misjudged him; I had mistaken his acts of kindness for weakness, and that would come back to bite me in the ass later in life.

My parents, still concerned about my arrogance and overwhelming determination to succeed at anything at any cost, decided to make a change in my social environment. They enrolled me in a Quaker School where I would begin my ninth grade, or as we knew it, high school years.

I was not amused or pleased at the prospects of being out of my element. There was something bazaar about this school, which dated back 100 years. It was old and anchored in the past on what they perceived as right and wrong. Far more liberal and permissive than what I was used to in Catholic School. The Quaker philosophy had few boundaries, so there would be little opportunity for exploitation. And it is exploitation that turns a profit. If I was not sure of anything else at that point, I was sure of that fact.

But going to a private school made my parents happy, and I thought I at least owed them that much. I decided to suck it up and hope for the best.

What the hell was I thinking!?

First day of school and orientation, what the hell is orientation? I already knew how to take care of myself. I was capable of finding the men's room and I knew how to tell time. *Was this bullshit really necessary,* I thought, *were they kidding?*

THE ANGLER IN THE SHADOWS

It didn't take long for me to size up the situation. The school was awash with kids from well to do families, spoiled and catered to most of their lives. They had no idea how to survive outside their little sheltered existence and most with no street smarts whatsoever. They were self-absorbed shits with attitudes and moral convictions based on nothing but their ability to buy their way out of uncomfortable situations.

To quote a line from the movie *My Blue Heaven*, **"Where others might see a problem, I see opportunity."**

I was the only Roman Catholic in the freshman class and the only Italian. I would hear the comments being made behind my back as I walked the halls, at lunch, and on Wednesday's when Quakers hold their reflection gathering at the Meeting Hall just down the street from the school.

There I sat in silence for the first few weeks. Then came my time. I began coming to school dressed the way I always did while hanging on the corners of some of the toughest streets in South Philly. If you listen to the words of the Billy Joel song, "Keeping the Faith," you will get the picture. Pompadour hair with shaved off side burns, velvet jacket with no collar, an iridescent shirt with a spaghetti neck tie and Matador boots, and an Italian switch blade tucked inside. I had not forgotten from whence I came and what I had learned from the days at the pool hall or walking tall with my Uncle Nick. I was a grenade waiting for someone to pull the pin, wanting someone to pull the pin. And someone did…

Someone sitting behind me during freaking meditation was telling another, "That's the Dago from South Philly in front of us, he thinks he's a hard ass." I can still recall the joy I felt in knowing I was about to convert the "he thinks," to "he is a hard ass."

With the speed of a punctured helium balloon, I turned, fists clinched, eyes focused on the area of this kid's face I wanted to cut. With the unrelenting repetition of an automatic weapon, I struck my target over and over until the anti-violence quack Quaker's leaped from the stage where they were seated in meditation to pull me off my prey.

The dye had now been cast. I was the kid to go to if you were a student who had a problem with one of the many arrogant upper classmen who felt picking on smaller kids was fun.

Needless to say, my classroom roster had been altered to reflect the Head Master's attempt to bring me into conformance with the school's liberal and passive views. Deep down we both knew there wasn't a snowballs chance in hell of that ever happening, so every day while the other kids had an academic class during third period, I had detention, which he called inner reflection. And so I reflected, how could I make a buck out of this situation? I already had the entire school's attention, now I needed a plan.

I came up with a great idea. I would sell protection. Protection from who, you might ask, in a school of non-violent activists, why, protection from me!

I went to my dad's office after hours and used his mimeograph machine to print out hundreds of leaflets with a representation of a black hand atop a phrase, reading "Five bucks a week and fear no one." I began to infiltrate the locker rooms at the school and slip in a pamphlet. It worked, and by the end of the first week, the money came in and it wasn't long before I was collecting about $300 a month. I also found a way into the assistant dean's office. I gained access to the file on student grades, and for a small fee, I could change any student grade on any subject.

I was in trouble with the Head Master on a regular basis, although each and every time he would meet with my parents, he told them how well I was doing and how much I was liked by the faculty. This of course was bullshit, and I told my parents if they did not get me out of there, something bad was going to happen.

By late October of my sophomore year, I was out and on my way to Bishop Neumann High, the school where I would have gone in the first place. I was back in Catholic School but not back in the faith.

1963-1965 the old Quaker School Library across from the school which was just as old. This was my refuge from attending the Quaker meetings when possible.

The Meeting House where I had to prove Italian guys from South Philly don't practice the virtue of "turn the other cheek"

1963-1966 High School Years This is the guy who you needed to pay for protection from other high school bullies. I didn't look anything like the other kids at the school, so it was easy to find the guy you had to pay!

AN EPIPHANY.

The influence of a man, a teacher, a friend and a priest! His name was Father La Luzerne and he was a St. Norbert Priest. He was a great guy and someone I came to admire.

He was there for me when I wanted to take certain math courses, I knew I would need to pursue my dream of attending an architecture college. Those higher math classes were not in my Class track, but he, as the instructor of those classes, convinced the dean to allow an exception. He also taught mechanical drawing, which was the precursor to drafting, another course I would need for the future.

He and I soon became close friends, and I visited him on numerous occasions after dinner at his rectory to discuss my life, my fears, my past experiences with abuse, and my latent anger with the church. We also talked for long hours about my lost faith. He listened but never pushed an agenda. I felt comfortable confiding my suppressed feelings with him.

As time went on, we developed a mutual confidence in each other, and I began to let go of my hate and again wanted to strive to be a better person and less indifferent to the needs of others. My family became fond of this gentle man, and he was present at many dinners and functions. We had become close friends, and he played a big part in my life.

All through the remaining time in high school, this closeness brought me an awareness of my spiritual side. Once again I felt complete and in control of my future. A calmness that would last into my college years, and although I fell along the way many times, I never was discouraged but kept a healthy perspective on my human weaknesses and accepted them for what they were.

My remaining years at Bishop Neumann High were rewarding; I could feel myself growing in many directions, and a newfound sense of freedom and independence gave me an unshakable level of self-confidence and power.

I must admit, the remorse I felt when I went astray was limited. I would try to do the right thing, but it didn't always work out that way. I enjoyed the pleasure derived from the lack of judgment. It was action without repentance made afterward.

In many ways, the days of my childhood while working the streets, making connections with powerful people, and the arrogance derived from those experiences were somehow slowly creeping back into my phyche.

I was a player among my peers and someone others seemed to gravitate to when there was a problem. I liked that feeling and did my best to help solve issues. Over time I had a group of guys who stuck together and traveled together outside school and on social gatherings.

It grew to be known as a group of tough guys not to be screwed with. Our gang would come to be known as the "Cross Men." In addition to the gold chain necklaces with a dangling Christian gold cross, we all had an additional chain hanging around our necks, it was the Maltese Cross, hence the gang name.

Bishop Newmann was located near the housings projects mostly inhabited by minorities and what we would call a low life element.

Back then you were identified by where your gang's corner was, for us it was 22nd and McKean. It was close to Neumann and not far from the Vare High School where most of the students came from the projects.

Neighborhoods were protected by the guys on the corners, and if you didn't belong in the area, you would be well-advised to walk around and find another way to get to where you were going. Our corner was no exception, and on many occasions, kids from Vare would test that rule, and on many occasions, there were violent classes, which resulted in beatings with bats and stabbings. Some guys even carried Zip Guns. To give the reader a visual of a Zip Gun, it's a wooden hand grip attached to a short piece of pipe, where a 22-caliber bullet was placed, a spring-loaded trigger with a nail would propel the bullet; it resembled a scene from *West Side Story*, but it was no musical, this was survival.

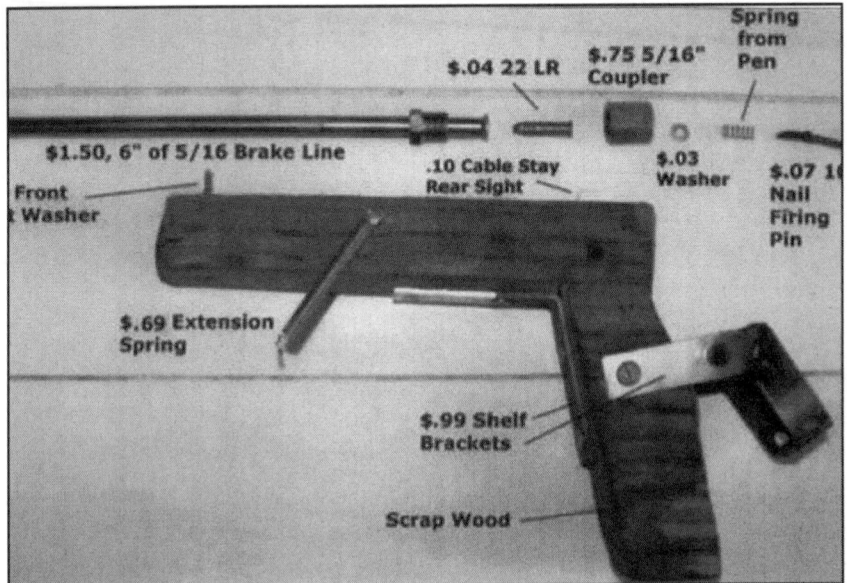

Street weapon called a Zip Gun This was common among gangs and was easily made using scarp metal It was capable of firing a 22-caliber long jacket bullet, one shot at a time, but was just as lethal as a manufactured hand gun. The instructions for making a Zip Gun are still available online today.

Keeping in mind that Bishop Neumann's attendees were about 98% Italian, it was a close nit group from freshman class to seniors. The school was all boys and total enrollment of about 3,000.

I recall the scene on St. Patrick's Day where the only green you could see was either on the floor, in the parking lot, or in a trash can.

But on St. Joseph's Day, which was two days later, the classes looked like a Mafia funeral, guys dressed in black suites, black shirts with white ties, and many even wore white carnations.

In South Philly, you could find on almost every corner a group of guys singing acapella and competing with other corner groups for recognition and prestige.

These same groups would also make the rounds to Saturday night dances throughout Philadelphia and South Jersey. They would occupy their own space within the dance hall, and everyone knew where the boys from South Philly were. They all could dance and sing and all the girls wanted to hook up with one of the guys. We had a reputation of being tough, but left alone, posed no threat; we were there for a good time, but make no mistake, if confronted or challenged, it didn't take long for a war to break out.

In time our reputation was so wide spread that if you were a group from South Philly, some dance halls would not let us in; that didn't work out well for the gate keepers of the dance hall as we were usually a group of about forty or fifty guys.

During the summer months, this whole scene would emerge at the Jersey Shore and the dance halls from Atlantic City to Wildwood. The Cross men gang had grown to about 100 guys and now came from as far away as New York to join up with us from June to September.

During the day and early evenings before the dance halls opened, the gang would hang out at the pool hall on Lincoln Avenue called the Miscue.

The pool hall was also frequently visited by large groups of sailors and Cost Guard cadets as the main training facility was located in Cape May.

I see great opportunity. In my early years, I learned a lot about playing pool from the Wise Guys at Jimmy's pool hall.

I am fifteen and appear to be of no threat to the transient sailors who have lots of money and time and like to challenge the local boys to a game of eight ball.

At first I would play coy and decline a challenge but in time would agree and slowly raise the stakes as the games went on until we were playing a game of eight ball for $100. Needless to say, on a good night, I could make about $500.

Even though they might have felt they were being hustled ,there was seldom a confrontation as there were always more of us than them at the pool hall.

The summer of my fifteenth year did not play out well for me. My dad, who became curious as to my whereabouts from early morning to late at night, began to quiz my friends. When he found out I was hustling at the pool hall, he showed up one day and pulled me outside and broke my custom-made pool cue and cautioned the manager not to let me hang out there anymore.

My daytime adventures were greatly curtailed, and I had only my nights at the Starlight Ball Room to look forward to.

That, too, would come to a sudden demise. One night while hanging with my group of Cross Men at the dance, a scuffle broke out with a group of guys from North Jersey over someone's girlfriend dancing with one of our gang. It quickly got out of hand, and we began throwing these guys over the deck railings, falling down about fifteen feet on the hard beach sand. The police were called and entered the dance in force, pulling our guys out onto the boardwalk and down to the police station.

I was collared by a cop, who I knew well, but it wasn't a Kumbaya relationship.

All this commotion had drawn a large crowd of spectators on the boardwalk as one by one our guys were dragged out. I was not so fortunate, as Sargent O'Shae was escorting my ass out, we ran directly into my parents, who were on the boardwalk watching what was unfolding. O'Shae, who knew my dad, presented my carcus in front of him and asked if he wanted to take me off his hands.

After a short pause, my dad looked at me and said, "No, take him with the others, it will teach him a lesson." And it did! The lesson learned was don't get caught!

At the police station, when my turn came to give an explanation, I could not help but mix my anger with sarcasm, and when asked if I had any identification, I looked in the nearby mirror and said, "Yep, that's me," and with a stern look on the desk sergeant's face, his reply was, "Cops do not have a sense of humor." I spent that night along with about ten of my friends sleeping in a cell until my dad came the next morning to drag my sorry ass out the door.

My dad brought me to the office of a builder whom he had real estate dealings with and told him I was now one of his new laborers until the end of the summer.

I spent the rest of those days installing fiberglass insulation in the crawl spaces of homes being built in Wildwood Crest. It was a shit experience, but I met some interesting construction workers, who to put it mildly, were freaking crazy. Hanging with them was even more dangerous than getting in fights at the Starlight Ball Room.

1965 August my 17th birthday at the Jersey Shore with my dad, brother, and grandfather. I am wearing a Maltese cross, this was one of my gang years.

June 1967 High school graduation

August 1967 My 19th birthday

CHAPTER SIX
Summer Of Independence

Its late June 1964, and once again, I am at the South Jersey Sea Shore. After my work experience with the local builder, I am re-hired and put on a work crew with the framers as a carpenter's apprentice and one of a five-man team.

Fred was the foreman, his son was a laborer, Danny was the nephew of the builder who did roofing and siding, Big Jim was the main carpenter, and I was his apprentice.

We had three houses to complete that coming season; work began at 6:30 A.M. until about 6:00 P.M. The work was rewarding but hard and demanding. I loved the challenge and the bond between myself and the team members.

Fred was a middle-aged, no-nonsense kind of guy who didn't say much and almost never smiled, but it was easy to tell when he wasn't happy with our work ethic. His son was called At-Water since he spent most of the day drinking from the job cooler. Big Jim was a tall, well-build black guy in his mid-thirties, Danny was late twenties, tall, toned, and crazy! I was of course still fifteen with my upcoming birthday coming on August 9th.

Everyone was pretty much normal, except for Danny, he was a Green Barret applicant who was rejected for reasons we never knew. He and I spent lots of time together, even after work. He confided in me that he was an active member of what was called the "Minute Men." That group of guys were the equivalent of what today we call

Dooms Day Preppers. It turns out they were also on the states list of organizations to watch. I soon would find out why.

One day after work was called off due to rain, we went to his apartment to hang out, waiting for the weather to change. Danny started to share with me the collection of weapons he had on hand waiting for a breakdown on civilization to occur.

He had hand guns, bowie knives, bayonets, and an assortment of rifles, among them an M-1 Carbine, converted to fully automatic machine gun, a military surplus from the Korean War, he had a crate of .30 caliber bullets arranged in thirty-round banana clip magazines.

As if that wasn't scary enough, in his closet he had several hand-grenades and a snare used to decapitate almost anything. It is basically two pieces of round wooden handles with a three-foot piece of piano wire strung between them. By looping the wire around any soft object, like someone's neck, and pulling sharply on the handles in opposite directions, you could kill someone instantly. *Yuck*, I thought, *this guy was dangerous!*

Thankfully the rain stopped and we were able to get the hell out of his apartment and go back to work. I was happy to be back on the job. Jim asked where I went off to.

I told him what happened and he shook his head and said, "Yeah, stay away from Danny; he is definitely not too stable."

With a smirk on my face, I look at Jim and say, "Now you tell me."

Several days go by, and we are now working on the second house to be framed this summer. It's about ninety-five degrees and humid; to keep from getting heat-stroke, Fred tells us we are cutting the day short. It's about two in the afternoon, and I need to find a way to cool off.

Danny says, "Let's go over to Sunset Lake and jump off the dock into the bay." We pack up our tools and we drive over to the bay in his car.

The guy who owns the dock is a friend of my dad and goes by the name of D. He lets us walk out to the end of the fishing dock to jump in and cool off. About 100 yards out from the dock is a floating fancy-looking barge that D rents out for a small fee to tourists. Danny wants to swim out to it, but out of courtesy, I think we should ask permission, so we do and D says no, he rented to a couple for a picnic and they would be arriving shortly.

Danny starts to argue with him, but I give him a nudge and say let's go. D has been kind enough, and I don't want to take advantage of his kindness.

Danny and I part ways, but I can tell he is still pissed about the barge. I don't think much about it, but in my gut, I have an uneasy feeling about this crazy guy.

It's now about 11 P.M., and I am getting ready for bed; we start work at 6 A.M. and it comes early when you're tired from the day before.

As I am getting into bed, I hear sirens in the distance. The lake is only two blocks from my house, and I hear the sounds getting closer and closer. I run to the door and can see the flashing red lights parked near D's dock, and looking out at the bay, I can see the flames lurching from the fancy barge. A marine police boat is out there as well, trying to put the fire out; it doesn't look promising.

I have a feeling inside; I know what happened. Danny swam out in the dark and blew up the barge. I hope I am wrong, but I can't think of any other possibility.

As thing calm down, it's approaching, 1 a.m. and I need some sleep. In the morning, when I get to the job, everyone is talking about the incident from the previous night, everyone that is except for Danny. He didn't show up for work, and Fred hasn't heard from him or his uncle about Danny's whereabouts.

Hours pass and finally Fred tells us Danny will be back tomorrow, but no other explanation is offered and we don't ask. I tell Jim of my suspicion, and we both think Danny was picked up for questioning, but because of this family connections, they probable let him go with a warning. I tell Jim I wouldn't be surprised if tomorrow we are building a barge to replace the one that was blown up.

The rest of the day passes without incident, and with a sigh of relief, I pack my tools and head for home to get some sleep and try to catch up from the night before.

Morning comes at the clang of my alarm, and I am here alone. My mother has gone back to Philadelphia and will come back this weekend with my dad and brothers.

I am old enough to be here unsupervised, and with trepidation from my dad, he has given me some rope hoping I won't use it to hang myself.

I am enjoying the freedom and don't want to screw things up by being involved in any crazy shit; Wildwood Crest is a small place and rumors spread quickly. My dad is well-known here and that makes things even more difficult. I eat, sleep, and work and that's about it.

After a quick bowl of cereal and a cup of coffee, I walk over to the job site. It's early, and Fred is the only one there so far. I say good morning and go about my business without any mention of Danny.

By 6:30 everyone is on the job, including Danny. Work begins as usual with Jim and I on the roof installing plywood and Fred setting up interior walls, Danny is setting up for siding, and At-Water is, well, you can guess where he is now.

Things are going smoothly as we approach lunch time, and we are all coming down for our break. By 12:30 we are back to our tasks. Danny is climbing back on his scaffolding when we hear a loud crash and yelling from Danny, who is holding his arm and climbing back to the ground. Before we know what is happening, Danny goes to the trunk of his car and emerges with the M-1 I mentioned earlier; standing back from the house, he begins to spray the side of the house with a barrage of bullets, wood and siding is flying everywhere. I jump out the window opening, and Jim jumps off the roof, which is two stories off the ground. Fred runs over to tackle Danny and stop the craziness before someone gets killed.

In a flash, the area is surrounded by police and quickly take Danny in cuffs and throw him in the back of a police car. We, along with all the immediate neighbors, are standing in shock wondering what the hell just happened.

Needless to say, that was the end of the day's construction progress. The whole side of this house will have to be rebuilt, and I don't think we are going to meet the summer schedule.

I am asking myself why am I thinking about that when I just witnessed one of the most insane scenes I ever saw, and to think I was part of the drama and what horror could have unfolded. I knew when my parents got here this weekend, my summer job would be over.

What would I do now, how would I get through the rest of the summer? I knew for sure there is no way they would let me stay here alone and would most likely drag my ass back to the city. My sixteenth birthday is only two weeks away, and I would be able to take my driving test. If I pass on my first try, maybe I could at least go visit some of my friends and have somewhat of a decent remainder of summer before school starts again.

The trauma of today's events will remain in my memory for some time to come. The possession of an M-1 carbine and its power will play a role in my future but not considered in my mind at this time. I was focusing on my immediate future right now.

And just as I suspected, my parents' arrival that weekend was tense. They had already heard of the incidents of the past week and were concerned as to what consequences might arise out of an ongoing investigation and if in any way I might be involved.

After several conversations with Danny's father and members of the local police, my dad was convinced I had no part in the carnage, but to keep it that way, they thought it best to ship me back to the city the following week.

CHAPTER SEVEN
Mobility And Freedom

It's now mid-August, back in South Philadelphia, and have reached my sixteenth birthday. Along with that milestone came the ability to study for and take my driver's license test.

With the help of my buddy Lou, who acted as my driving instructor, began the task of guiding me around the obstacles and skills I would need to master at the DMV while taking my driving test. At that time, the test was regulated by the PA State Police, and from what Lou told me, there was no leeway, you either passed or failed.

Growing up among the small streets of South Philly and navigating through them, some no wider than the width of a car, plus a few feet, driving down them came easily.

Next Lou and I ran the gambit of traveling one of the busiest streets in the city, Broad Street; we traveled from the southern most part, going north around the city hall circle, continuing north to the end, turned around, and headed back to our beginning.

Next was the final test, getting on what is known as the Schuylkill Expressway, known to the locals as the Surekill Expressway. I knew if I could successfully make that trip, I would be ready for any test they could administer.

Success. I completed every challenge Lou put me through, and with a cocky smile on my face, walked in on my dad and told him I was going to the DMV tomorrow with Lou to take my driving test. My dad put the newspaper down and told me I was crazy; I only had my learners permit for two days. There is no way I could pass the exam with that little experience. So I put forward a wager. If I passed my exam, could I have the car that Friday night. My dad, feeling this was an easy bet, agreed.

My older brother Bill, however, wasn't so happy with the prospects of the outcome. He already had his driver's license and was accustomed to having access to my parents' second car on the weekend; if I passed the exam, that would all change and we would from that day forward have to share that car on weekends.

The next morning, Lou and I are at the DMV at 8:45 A.M., fifteen minutes before it opened, so we could get an early appointment.

The doors open, and I am the third in line. First there is a verbal exam given by a tester where you are asked at least twenty questions from the Driving Manual I got with my permit. You can't take the driving test if you don't pass the verbal portion.

I get every question right, and she stamps my ticket and directs me to the lot to take the driving test. My name is called over a megaphone, and a stern-looking trooper takes my card, looks at the dates, and asked if I really think I am ready given the short amount of time I had the permit.

I look him square in the eye and reply, "No sweat, I got this." He doesn't seem amused and tells me to get in the driver seat, he sits in the passenger seat with a clipboard and tells me to proceed to the first orange cone.

After about twenty minutes and an equal amount of driving maneuvers, my instructor looks down at his clipboard, makes a few entries, then looks over at me with a smirk and says, "You passed, kid, take this paper inside and they will give you your driver's license."

With a well-deserved swagger, I walk inside where Lou is waiting to hear. I wave the certificate in the air, and Lou give me a thumbs up and goes out to wait for me at the car, now parked in the licensed drive only parking lot.

Leaning on the fender of my mom's Pontiac LeMans, Lou has this big shit-eating grin on his face and walks over and gives me pat on the back, now switching rolls from instructor to passenger, we get on the Schuylkill Expressway and head back home.

It's Friday morning, and I want to confirm my deal with my dad about this evening before he heads off to his office and before my brother Bill makes a claim for himself for that evening.

As I walk into our kitchen, my mom is setting out a breakfast plate for Lou and I, my dad is sipping on his coffee. I am standing in front of him as he looks up with a "I told you so" look on his face. With a smirk, I pull my newly minted Driver's License from behind my back.

Before he can say anything, I say, "So is six o'clock okay to take Mom's car?"

My dad is perplexed, and my mom looks over at him with a smile and says, "Were you expecting something different?" She looks over at me and says six o'clock is ok with her. Since it's her car, I take that as a YES.

My dad rises from his chair puts on his suit coat and says, "a deal is a deal," kisses my mom, and leaves for his office.

Lou and I are eating so fast, we are barely taking time to chew; we are discussing what we want to do that evening to celebrate my good fortune. First things first, back then no self-respecting teenager would be caught on the road in a car that wasn't squeaky clean and smelled of pine trees in the interior.

After we finish breakfast, Lou says, "Good bye, see you tonight," and leaves for his house around the corner.

My younger brother Bruce now comes down to the kitchen and asks what's going on. I wave my new license in his face and tell him to get dressed and we can take a ride down to the park and drive around to show off.

Bruce is seven year younger than I, so he doesn't yet get the level of importance of the event but sees my excitement and rushes off to get dressed. By three o'clock, we are back in the driveway, breakout the necessary cleaning supplies needed to convert a mom car into a **"PLAYERS"** car.

By 6 P.M., my chariot is sparkling, and you could eat off the fenders. I am dressed and ready to go. I call over to Lou's house and tell him I'll be there shortly.

I say good bye to my mom, and she reminds me I have to be home before midnight as my new license required it, they are known as a "Cinderella" license. I pull in front of Lou's house and give a quick beep of the horn. He is out in less than a minute, and we are off to where? We have no idea, just being able to drive is an adventure all its own.

We pick up a few of our buddies and decided to head over to Mount Laurel, New Jersey, where in the middle of a farm field there is a malt shop known as the Cow Tail Bar, a hang-out frequented by teenagers from all over the area, and there are especially lots of farm country girls, a jukebox in the corner, and a dance floor. There are competing gangs of guys from different towns but never is there any physical conflict; we all know that would ban all of us from this place for sure. So peace usually prevails, that is a welcome environment, especially for guys from South Philly, no threats and nothing to prove, just music, dancing, flirting, and lots of ice cream.

I felt a new sense of being, I was coming into my own, developing a new persona, expanding my horizons and widening my circle of friends. It was my first night out in control of my own destiny, or so it seemed. This might just be a false euphoria, but I just accepted it for what it was and enjoyed the feeling on the ride home.

I arrived home about 11:20 P.M. only to find my parents and brother Bill waiting up for me, just making sure I got back without incident and before midnight. I wasn't going to kill my chances of getting the car next week by being stupid.

My brother Bill and I shared the same room, and as I was getting ready for bed before shutting the light, he looked over and said, "I am glad everything worked out okay tonight, hope you had a good time."

"Thanks," I said. "I'll tell you all about it tomorrow."

It's Saturday morning, August 15th, 1964 about 8 A.M., sitting at the kitchen table with my brother Bill having breakfast. I was telling him about the previous night's activities at the Cow Tail Bar, he knows the place and has been there many times with his own group of friends. Bill and I are only seventeen months apart, and even though we have some of the same friends, due to growing up in a small neighborhood, but for the most part, due to high school, we have our own circle of close friends.

We both knew we would have to come up with an agreeable solution to the car issue, or we would be at odds every week trying to get possession of the extra car.

To resolve the issue, we agree on alternating each week on who would have access on Friday night and who would have it on Saturday, the next week we would switch; on Sunday's similar arrangement, one would have it in the morning until 2 P.M. and the other from 2 P.M. to 8 P.M. We both feel this would be the most equitable solution and let our parents know what we came up with. They are amazed we came up with a solution on our own but think it's a great idea and approve.

My mom yells in to me that Lou is on the phone. Good thing he called, as mentioned earlier, it is common place that in South Philly there are a number of Italian guys on corners to form a-cappella groups singing what today is known as Doo Wop. We have a confirmed spot at a nearby community center, known as the Reed House, to perform that evening.

To paint a mental picture of what this was like, there were four of us in the group, Lou, Joey, Alfred, and myself. Joey picked the songs and made copies of the lyrics of the songs we practiced and sang at events. Lou and Al sang back up with Joey and I sang lead. We dressed in conformity with black slacks, matador black boots, white collared shirt, and baby blue V-neck button down sweaters.

That afternoon we spent several hours practicing the two songs we were scheduled to perform, it's funny that even today I remember the songs and still sing them in my head on occasion when I am driving alone. "Pennies From Heaven" and "Blue Moon." I am smiling now even as I write this paragraph.

We are back stage now listening to other groups perform, waiting for our introduction to walk out.

Finally the MC calls for the lights to dim and tells the audience, "The next group has performed many times at clubs in the area but were able to get us here tonight for their enjoyment, please welcome The Chessmen." We take our place on stage and the house lights come on, we are standing with our arms folded in front and our heads bowed down.

There are about 100 teenagers in the audience, mostly girls. The audience is quiet, and looking up slowly, I begin to sing with Lou, Joey, and Al now singing backup. The girls start to cheer, and we go into our choreography all perfectly timed and performed.

We have done this many times before and enjoy the bookings but realize in the era of the Beatles, a-cappella is a fading form of entertainment, besides we are all beginning to gravitate toward other and different interests, mostly around cars and girls. No surprise there!

Lou and I, however, continue to hang out. Not far from where we live in a large multi city block area is the Food Distribution Center, there is a wide road between the huge warehouses meant to accommodate tractor trailers stretching close to a quarter mile, straight run with no obstacles. Perfect for drag racing, and on Friday and Saturday nights, when the warehouses were closed, dozens of hot rods and supped up stock cars would line up for races. Some for money and some for recognition.

Lou's sister just got a new car, a Chevy Nova, which was a compact model, but he persuaded her to order as an upgrade, a larger than standard engine with a four-barrel carburetor. Unbeknownst to her, with his setup, if you hit the gas pedal from a dead stop, the front end would come off the ground and the rear tires would vigorously spin for traction going from zero to sixty miles per hour in a matter of seconds, perfect for drag racing.

Not to be left out of this new exciting pastime, my brother Bill and I proceed to transform our mom's LeMans from a stock version to a drag version.

With the help of a buddy who works at an auto mechanics garage, we remove the intake manifold with its stock two-barrel carburetor and installed a new intake manifold with twin four-barrel carburetors. That improvement alone would increase the horse power three-fold. In addition my brother had the duel exhaust manifold cut and welded two bypass vents with removable caps that would allow the exhaust to exit the engine before the mufflers, and with the caps removed, would increase the horse power by another twenty. This previous stock car is now a race car.

We ran and won races on the strip time after time, and our car became well known. After months of enjoying the attention, things took a turn we did not see coming. My mom had been complaining to our dad that her car was running strange and she did not feel safe driving it around town. After driving it himself, he agreed that something wasn't right and made an appointment at the dealership to have it checked out.

After sitting in the dealership waiting room for a few hours, the head mechanic comes out and asked them if they have any teenage drivers at home, to which they reply, "Two, why?" He tells them the car has been modified and their sons are racing this car.

Needless to say, that evening after dinner, conversation went from mild to frantic; after hours of condemnation we were told to put the car back to the way it was at our expense and banned from us driving for a month.

That was the end of our drag racing days, which was just as well since now the police were aware of the strip and showed up in force issuing tickets to all drivers who showed up.

These antidotal stories may seem irreverent to the book but play a significant part in my adulthood development.

CHAPTER EIGHT
The Domino Effect

Summer is now over, and with September comes the beginning of my junior year at Bishop Neumann where I will once again be reacquainted with my homeroom classmates. Nothing changes in Catholic school. Your homeroom is set the first day of your freshman year and arranged in alphabetical order, and your classmates will be the same until the day you graduate.

Some of my mates have been hanging with me during the summer, so we are sharing our adventures with others comparing experiences.

Our homeroom monitor is Father Frigo, he is a Norbertine Priest and speaks Italian and broken English. He was born and raised in Italy and comes from a wealthy family who produces many types of cheeses shipped around the world. He is a mild manner man of stocky build and with a good sense of humor. Nothing is taught in homeroom, it's like a staging area when our group gathers for morning prayer and attendance prior to the first period bell. Hearing it ring, we are all off to different classes, running halls and floors to get to the next period before the bell. Those who do not make it in time are locked out of class only to be confronted by walking hall monitors who require you to produce a hall pass, without which you are given a detention slip as punishment; after five detention slips, you will have to show up on a Saturday morning and remain in study hall in silence until 2 P.M. That sucks and resembles the movie *Breakfast Club*. I have found myself there on several occasions, it sucks.

My third period is Geometry, followed by fourth period, which is Mechanical Drawing; it's in the same classroom with the same priest, Father La Luzern. He and I are friends, he helped me jump classes and tracks, which takes an act of God or dispensation from the Pope under normal circumstances. My college plan is to study Architecture and I would need very specific classes and grades on my high school transcript to even apply to a college.

For me it meant jumping around from track to track to get the classes I needed. I am in debt to this priest as it could not have been accomplished without his help.

Junior year is now in full swing, along with social activities, which include Saturday night dances. The same group of my buddies from Wildwood's Starlight Ballroom are always there and the girls from Saint Marie Goretti, which is an all-girl high school, are always in attendance. During the summer at Starlight, I earned a moniker for changing the lyrics of songs to a more graphic sexual interpretation, along with my style of dance, to "Bobby Sex." It kind of stuck and followed me back to the dances at Newmann; it was kind of cool having a nickname others used to identify me with when I showed up. Guys and girls alike would shout it out when certain songs would be played by the disk jockey.

Father La Luzern was a regular chaperone at the dances and would walk around to couples dancing, and if they were too close, he would say, "Back up and leave room for the Holy Ghost." He was comical. Whenever he sees me, he would come over and whisper in my ear, "Bobby, your pants remind me of a cheap hotel, no ball room!"

"Funny," I would tell him; he would just smile a walk away.

Christmas break is coming, and along with it, mid-term exams. This year was extremely important to do well as the grades attained would be sent to any prospective college and play into the tiers set up for the SAT's.

The grades come out, I did great; things are starting to fall into place one after the other, and I am feeling blessed. School is out for the holiday break, and I am looking for another way to make money, in addition to hustling at Mosconi pool hall. Next door there is a men's clothing store called Slacks and Jacks. They are looking for part-time help, so I apply. The clothes they sell are nothing I would wear, it's geared for an older crowd. My mom always took us to Arnold's Men's Shop on Passyunk Avenue for clothes. The style and quality of their selection was geared for the discriminating Italian male, shark skin suits, silk shirts and ties, and accessories straight from Milan, Italy. This is where the local Wise Guys shopped; on many occasions while we were there, I would recognize some faces from my shoe shine days.

That is how I was dressed when I applied for the job. The manager was a young Italian guy from the neighborhood.

He took one look at me and said, "ARNOLD'S?" with a smile.

"Yep," I said.

He laughed and said, "We don't carry anything like that here, but you make a great first impression. When can you start?"

"Today," I replied.

"Okay, Bobby $4 an hour, plus commission of six percent."

With that motivation, I put a smile on my face and greeted the first customer through the door. By the time I was done upselling, he was ringing up everything from underwear to a three-piece suit. Antonio was the inhouse tailor and began showing me how to mark-up alterations myself when he wasn't there. That made the clothing ready for pick-up faster and that meant I got my commission faster. Needless to say, I was a quick learner. I made good money there and stayed on through the end of the school year.

Holidays are over and back to school. I had a great time working, making money, and buying gifts for my family. Again things are going my way one after the other.

Saturday night, January 30th, 1965. I am at Neumann dance in my comfort zone with my friends, both male and female. Father La Luzern is there as usual, still giving me the same wise ass remarks, but I know it's all in good fun. He always has my back!

It's about 10 P.M. when out of nowhere, my brother Bill walks in with Kenny, the son of my dad's good friend from the Army. I am in the middle of a slow dance with one of the usual girls from Goretti.

Billy taps my shoulder and says, "You have to go."

"Go where?" I said.

"To Kenny's house."

"Why?" I retort.

"It's his graduation party from Southern High, and his cousin Donna is there and he wants you to meet her."

"Are you guys nuts? I am not leaving."

"Yes, you are," and they grab my arms and drag me out to the parking lot.

"I don't get it, what's this really about? Who is she, what's she like, where she from? Is she Jive or Conservative?" Jive means you are cool, street smart, and dress the trend, conservative means penny loafers with white socks, button up white shirt with plaid skirt, and a virgin pin holding the skirt flap together.

"Jive," my brother tells me.

I shoot back, "Where she from?"

"West Philly," he says.

"Okay, I'll go but no promises."

I don't date girls from South Philly, too cocky, gruff, and always quick to give you some shit. It's like dating one of the guys on the corner, sometimes it's hard to tell the difference. The only way to find a nice girl from down town, as South Philly is known, is to meet her at a family function or church, but then you would have her family and your family following you around on dates, too much work, not worth it to me. I like my private life staying private.

We walk in, and within seconds, Kenny's father Jim grabs me and pulls me over to his niece Donna, pushing me closer to her.

He says, "This is Bobby, Billy's brother, he wanted to meet you."

"What the hell," I say to myself, "real slick, Jim, I am capable of my own introductions."

"Hi," she says. "I heard you just came from a school dance."

"Well, something like that," I reply. "Why are you here?"

"Well, Kenny is my cousin and I kind of didn't have a choice."

Softly I say, "Yeah, I get it." They are playing music, and I ask her to dance, one song after the other. I notice she is wearing desert boots same as I am; that is what most jive kids wore to a dance, suede half boots with rubber soles, easy to dance on. It's now midnight, and people are leaving the party, and I admit I didn't want to leave her, something inside clicked.

How can this be, I thought, in an instant everything seems to have changed, priorities, scheduled meeting with friends, commitments, and even work schedule. All gone from my conscious mind drifting instead to thoughts of how and when I could see her again. My mind is racing for a strategy as I drive home.

Back in our room, my brother and I are talking about the party and he says, "Aren't you glad we came to get you at the dance?"

"Yes," I say with a smile, "you guys just caught me off guard."

"So what did you think about meeting Kenny's cousin Donna?"

Scratching my head as I get in bed, I tell him, "I know it sounds crazy, but I think I am going to marry that girl!"

"You're crazy," he tells me and turns off the light.

Sunday, crack of dawn, I am the only one up, showered, dressed, and down stairs pondering what to do, where should I go to find her, and what would I say if I did?

Sometimes you just have to say what the hell and take your best shot. It's my turn with the car, so I grab the keys and head over to Kenny's house. It's only 8:30 A.M. and not much movement in the neighborhood. I park my car and walk up to the house, knock on the door, and wait, holding my breath, not knowing who would answer the door; maybe it will be her, then what?

The door swings open, and Ken's mom Lina says with a smirk, "HI, Bobby, are you looking for Ken?"

"No," I reply, but I sense she know that and makes me admit I was looking for her niece Donna.

"Did she know you were coming for her?"

"No," I reply, "I was wondering if maybe I could take her to church, the nine o'clock mass maybe!"

"Well, she is not here," my heart sinks, then she says, "She slept over her friend's house Nancy who lives next door. Why don't you come back in an hour and I'll call over and let her know you will be coming back to take her to church."

"Swell, I'll be back then," get back in my car and head home since it's only a few blocks away.

Like clockwork I am back at Ken's house by 9:30 and again knock on the door. This time Donna's mom Mary answers with a stern look on her face and asks where I was thinking on taking her daughter.

"Church," I reply, "it's only around the corner." Donna's uncle Jim chimes in from the kitchen that I come from a really good family and he has always known me to be a respectful kid, and Donna will be safe with me.

With that Mary steps aside and Donna comes to the door. She smiles and says hello, reaches out her hand, and steps out of the doorway.

"Don't be long," her mom says, and we are off to church. Everyone is watching as I open the passenger side door for my soon to be girlfriend. We wave good bye and head for church. I spent the entire time at mass staring at her, didn't hear one word the priest said, and missed communion completely.

I just wanted it to end, so I could spend time with Donna, drive to the nearby park, and get to know her a little better and see if she liked me as much as I liked her. I got the impression she did. After about an hour or so, I had to bring her back to where I know would be her anxious, over protective mom.

I park in front of the house. Mary is already standing at the front door. I gather all the nerve I can muster and ask if I could maybe see her next weekend for a date to a movie or malt shop near where she lives.

She smiles back at me and says, "That would be great." I help her out of the car and begin walking her to her aunt's front door;

now I realize that even though I am wearing my desert boots, it doesn't feel like my feet are touching the ground.

I thank her mom, aunt, and uncle for the previous night's party invite and tell Donna it was a pleasure meeting her and how much I am looking forward to seeing her again next weekend. She smiles, but her mom is not smiling, glances over at her daughter. I turn and walk out, leaving Donna to explain the arranged date night to her mom later.

The following week was the longest in my life. I called to talk to Donna every night after dinner counting the days and hours until our arranged date Friday night at seven.

Finally I am flying up the expressway to meet her, knocking on her front door with trepidation, not quite knowing what to expect from her parents. Her dad answers and welcomes me in; he is a tall, slender man with dark hair and tanned skin. He is a bricklayer and works outside, which explains his complexion. He reaches out to greet me with one hand and a bottle of beer in the other. Her mom says hello and yells up to Donna that I am here. My eyes are fixated on the stairway as she walks down. We both pause in our greeting, not sure if we should kiss hello, so we skip it. I address her dad and tell him I was thinking of going to the Hot Shop at 69th and Market Street, where you park and a waitress on roller skates comes over to take your order and return with a tray that attached to the driver side car window with all the burgers, fries, and milkshakes you can order.

For me it's like a fairytale date. I am sure I have found the girl I was meant to be with the rest of my life. I am a man of decision and single mindedness. I am not going to let this girl out of my life. My heart is pounding as we chow down on our meal, the radio is playing rock n' roll tunes, and my mind is formulating the words I want to say before I take Donna back home.

We are having a great time, and it all seems so natural, like we have known each other all our lives.

"This feels right," I tell myself and continue to repeat it in my head all the way back to Lotus Road where I know I must say goodnight. I park but not in front of her house. I look for a spot further down the street where her parents can't see us. I look over at her and move in closer to kiss her. She kisses me back, we linger for some time, and with a mutual hug, stare into each other's eyes. I speak first and tell her how I feel and know this is meant to be.

I swallow hard and ask, "Would you like to go steady with me?" She hugs me again and says yes. I am on cloud nine and not sure what to do or say. We kiss again and exit the car to greet her waiting family, now including her little sister Joann, cute little girl with long blond hair and slender build.

I stay for a short time but know I must be back by midnight, and it's about an hour to get home.

Her parents had the courtesy to retire to the second floor, which I am positive was her dad's idea, saying, "Good night, and be careful driving home." I give Donna a hug and kiss her good night, telling her I will call her in the morning to arrange when we can get together again.

This is a whole new experience for me, never had this feeling before about anyone. It's like a thirst you just can't seem to quench. It's like breathing, a function you need to perform but have no control over it, and every time I think of her, I automatically smile. I guess for a lack of any other explanation this must be what you call LOVE.

This girl, DONNA, is bound to change my life for the better and allow me to reach new heights and hopefully become the man I was destined to be. Yep, like domino's, piece by piece the chips of my life are continuing to fall in a positive direction. Can't wait to see where this road leads but as a team, a couple, hand in hand together.

CHAPTER NINE
Stronger Than Ever

Junior year is quickly coming to an end. Lots going on, Ring Dance, SAT's, and Junior Prom. Donna is my constant companion and the love of my life. She brings me peace, confidence, (not that it's an issue with me) but encouragement to keep following my dreams. Everything I do is to win her approval and pride in me. I never want to take that for granite or diminish the faith and trust she has in me.

And so I never look back, always forward, always positive, but the things I learned on the street from those who are always looking for and angle are always in the back of my mind. Always looking for an advantage, looking out for me first and living by the Silver Rule, the Golden Rule, doesn't work for me. The Silver Rule is "Do unto others first, before it is done unto you." I know that sounds harsh. Watching my dad while I was young and watching him let others sometimes take advantage really pissed me off; he would tell me kindness is not a sign of weakness, nevertheless I just could not relate. I think I got that from listening to my mother tell stories of how she had to constantly fight for what she wanted, and just because she was a girl, let that prevent her from obtaining what was rightfully hers.

My dad's family was a little more well off than my mom's, their background was that of formal education and exposure to higher social events. My mom's family was of the working-class; her mother was a farm worker and her dad, a common laborer. How my parents met at a dance and fell in love is an enigma to this day.

It is a constant moral struggle to keep both sides of my personality in check and play the right card at the right time. A high wire act for sure, but I am managing.

Ring Dance is spectacular, and when Donna and I walk in, she steals the show, but it's a dance, however, and my junior classmates know me well, along with the ever-present chaperones. Father La-Luzern approaches, and I introduce him to my girl Donna.

He smiles and tells me how lucky I am but leans over to Donna and says, "Keep your boyfriend in check, he has a wild side."

The night is spectacular and ends in a high note. We all know Junior Prom is not far off and will be the end of our junior year social events before the summer break.

Prom night finally arrives, and again couples are making arrangements on who to take to the prom, where to go after prom, how you make your entrance both from the drive up to the prom location and when you first walk into the room with your date. I have Donna, so most of those issues for me are moot.

On arrival Donna is stunning as usual, and I am proud to be with her. It is custom to show up at the girl's house for family pictures first, then the boy's house, each location full of family and friends with flashing cameras and well wishes by the hundreds. We arrive at the Neumann Auditorium, quickly unite with our close-knit group, and the dance comes off like clockwork. Life is moving swiftly, but when you're young, you never seem to notice. It's true when they say youth is wasted on the young.

With SAT's completed and exams shortly on the horizon, it's time to decide what colleges I want to apply for admission. I am firmly focused on the career of architecture, and Temple University is my first choice. Application complete and submitted, along with my junior transcript and SAT results, all I need do now is wait. I know I won't hear anything until fall, so I plan for what I will do this summer.

As much as I am looking forward to working again as a construction worker at the South Jersey Shore, I am not feeling good about not being able to see Donna for long stretches of time. I would come home some weekends and hope her parents would allow her to visit our shore house where my parents would be present and we will have supervision. The dye is cast, so all I can do is let things play out and hope for the best.

School is out, and I am at the Jersey Shore working in construction, but now I am a full-fledged carpenter. Donna is working part-time jobs back home, and we are able to switch off on occasion from my going home and her coming to the shore. We write letters to each other on a daily basis, and I still have every one she wrote, even today. It's fun to go back and read our adolescent scribblings and smile at how wide-eyed with promise we seemed back then.

My birthday is close, and Donna has made plans to be at the Shore for that weekend. I know she has been saving money all summer for something special and I am anxious for the day to arrive. It is the weekend of my birthday, and Donna is coming down the shore with my parents. I can't wait for her to get here as it's been several weeks since I saw her last.

My parents have plans for dinner and a small party with family and local friends to mark the celebration. Dinner is special as usual; my mom and aunt prepared all day with a multi-course meal followed by coffee and my favorite vanilla layered pound cake with Italian cream between the layers and vanilla butter cream frosting. I open all the cards and gifts with Donna's being the last to be opened, and to my surprise, she had a custom two-piece pool stick made for me. I can't stop smiling knowing how expensive this gift was but figure I can make lots of money at the pool hall in town. Later that evening, my dad askes to see the pool stick, so I put the two pieces together and hand it to him; he remarks how great it looks but warns me not to start hustling at the pool hall because one day I am going to run into someone like my Uncle Nick, who won't be happy losing money to some wise ass kid with a custom pool stick.

He hands it back to me and says, "Enjoy it."

The weekend is over ,and my parents are headed back to Philly with Donna, and I am sad to see her go, but in a few weeks, summer will be over and I will be home for good. Senior year, college prep, and decisions that will set the stage for life long choices. Can't help but ponder am I ready, have I prepared well enough, am I mature enough? I swallow hard and tell myself I am, I am, and I am. Now go let the world know you are here to kick ass and take names.

When I finally get back home, I have a surprise birthday gift waiting for me. It's from my Uncle Bob, who is married to my dad's sister Mary. He was as Master Sargent in the Marine Corps. Last winter he invited me to go with him to his gun club where he is an instructor at the big boar range; it's set up for only high-power rifles. He still looks like a Marine, short cropped hair cut, strong physique, and Gung-Ho. I loved being there with him and learned how to handle and respect the power and danger of weapons. The gift I unwrap is a war surplus military M-1 semi-automatic carbine with a bayonet and several multi round magazines for 30-caliber bullets, but none were included in the package. My dad is not pleased; since the war, he has had a dislike for guns and weapons. After calling my uncle, he is somewhat satisfied that I will only bring it to the gun club to use under strict supervision. I am so excited with the gift and look forward to going to the club. This will all play a part in the year soon to come.

It's now my first day back at school, it's my senior year, I am now one of the big shots on campus. It's not just me but the entire senior class, it's an unwritten respect given by the under classmen; we've been through it all and we have earned the respect of being seniors.

I am laser focused on my class selections and the grades I need, especially in the first semester as it is those grades on which college applications are judged. I am doing well, and with letters of recommendation from the Bishop Neumann Principal and my student counselor, I submit my resume. Several weeks later, I receive a letter from Temple University asking to schedule a face to face interview with the dean of the Architecture School for possible admittance.

The day of my interview arrives, and my mind is racing as I drive to the university; it's right on Broad and Colmumbia Avenue in North Philadelphia.

In my head, I am mentally going through the answers to questions I have not yet heard. I can do this, I tell myself, you have been through tough situations before, be yourself and remember what you learned from listening to conversations between my dad and some of his business partners.

"If you can't dazzle them with brilliance, baffle them with bullshit."

I'm here, sitting in the Dean's waiting room, waiting for him to call me into his office. He comes out to greet me, we sit and chat for a while. I figure he is trying to get some insight into my motivation and ability to apply myself and successfully complete the program. It goes well, and while we are finishing, he has one final question.

"Do you believe you can adjust to self-discipline and be able to self-motivate; this isn't high school, no one is pushing you to complete assignments or show up for class, it's a simple pass-fail environment."

"I can," I reply, :I always plan to succeed, and failure is never an option."

"I think you'll do well, Robert; you'll get your acceptance letter in a few weeks."

I can't wait to get home and surprise my folks with the good news and let Donna know I will be attending college next year at a local university, so we can see each other as often as we want.

There is one drawback. Temple is a great school but in a shit neighborhood, no way you would want to walk around the area at night or stray off campus. It's a low-life poverty area, my high school life is a similar situation but all the corner hang outs here are minority, no back up, no one to come to your aid if confronted. Now going back to the sixties, brought up in the inner city, racism and deep-rooted prejudice are common place and it cuts both ways, we hate them and they hate us, harsh, simple but a fact of life. You learn to deal with it and do whatever it takes to survive in the streets.

"I'll be fine," I tell myself, and go back to focusing on the positive aspects to tell my parents and Donna.

Relaying my good news to my buddies, I find out my friend Ralph has also applied and been accepted to Temple and in the same school as myself, but he is going to major in electrical design. We make plans to travel together taking turns on driving; it's an easy drive, straight up Broad Street, parking will be dicey, we will want to be as close to our building as possible and avoid isolated areas.

But those plans can wait. Senior Prom, exams, graduation, and summer break are all still ahead of me, and I know life will be moving at light speed.

A long-term plan is what is needed now if I want things to work out the way I envision. So it's "plan your work, then work your plan," good advice I learned somewhere along the way, can't remember where, but I'm using it now.

High school is now over, summer is just about over, and anxiety and anticipation begin to creep into my soul. The reality of what is coming begins to zoom in as September approaches. Ralph and I are setting up a schedule for the fall semester. We both have orientation the same day, again with the freaking orientation, but it's mandatory, so no skipping out on this one.

At least we get to meet some of the other students we will be sharing class with this semester. It's a riot, so many different groups of people, some from the area but most from other states and diverse backgrounds; it's kind of cool though learning the world doesn't end at Broad and South Street, which is the unofficial boundary between South Philadelphia and Center City. My grandfather would always tell me, if you can't find what you want before South Street, you don't need it; funny how some words of wisdom stick in your head.

Orientation is over, and all the text books needed for my classes have been purchased, can't believe how expensive books can be. I need to get a part-time job to help out my parents, it's not necessary, but it's the right thing to do.

Ralph and I are all set and looking forward to day one and new experiences. Now I am going prepared for anything; in the trunk of my car, I am carrying my M-1 rifle with two thirty-round magazines of ammunition, just in case we ever need to provide our own back up. Now Ralph is as street smart as myself and knows the drill. I am well aware of how bad things can get, it's kind of lawless in areas like this, it's better to explain why I shot him than listen to why he shot me. This is no fairytale, this shit is for real. I don't want a reader thinking any of this is made up for dramatization. It's real!

CHAPTER TEN
Going To The Chapel

September 1966, college formally begin, Stauffer Hall is where most of my classes are located, Mitten Hall is a few blocks north and it's where most social gatherings take place, as well as the location of the cafeteria. It's an older building steeped in history dating to the beginning of Temple back to its founding in 1884.

Some of my classmates are also from urban areas, and some are so naïve, they hang close to the city boys and walk around in total amazement at what inner city life is like. Two have confided they never saw black people before. I laugh in surprise and tell them never to walk alone; it scares the shit out of them, but it's advice well-taken.

The nation is deep in the Vietnam War, and many of my high school friends have been drafted into the military, some come home with disabilities, some in a box, and some not at all. It's a scary time to be a teenager, the military lottery system is in full swing and deferments are being eliminated one by one. Survival literally depends on the luck of the draw, every week a series of draft numbers are being called. If your number comes up, you go, no debate, no negotiations, you show up for departure or MP's show up at your door. I am lucky, college students are still exempt.

It's also the height of the hippy movement, flower children are everywhere, demonstrations are being stages every day in front of Mitten Hall, you can smell pot for blocks, some are walking around like zombies strung out on LSD or some other hallucinogenic drug of choice. Campus police man the doors to the Hall, keeping the draft dodgers and demonstrators out of the cafeteria.

A lightbulb goes off in my head. If hundreds of these hippies can't go inside for a sandwich, why not provide sandwiches outside! Again, like in my past, where others see a problem, I see opportunity.

I grab Ralph after class and let him in on my plan. Let's set up a folding table outside Mitten Hall and sell lunchmeat sandwiches and soda. We could get $2 for a sandwich and $1 a can of soda. Keep it simple, they are all ham and cheese on white bread and all Coke.

The next day, we set up shop on the sidewalk outside the Hall with 100 sandwiches and fifty cans of soda. We had to cut one of our classes to do it, but we sold out in less than thirty minutes and were able to break down our set up and still make it on time for the next scheduled class, but we made $250 in no time; our cost was about $50.00. It's a no brainer and better than any lecture we could have gotten from the business school.

We rush home after classes are out, and drive over to the local deli and order enough lunchmeat for 200 sandwiches and 100 cans of soda and tell the owner to set us up for the same order for the following day. When we set up in front of the Hall again, its 11 A.M. and a crowd is already waiting, same result this time. We don't even make it to thirty minutes as kids are buying multiple sandwiches and sodas. And again we still make our next scheduled class.

We have to step it up, this is a gold mine waiting to be tapped. Our deli order is now expanded to make at least 500 sandwiches with an equal compliment of soda. Ralph recruits his two aunts to help keep up with the demand. It's crazy as they are working until midnight or later to get what we need. We are now paying his aunts for the help and his cousins are chipping in. We raise our prices by a dollar for both items and usually sell out within an hour or so, but now we are missing two classes a day, and our professors are getting pissed at our constant absence.

This endeavor goes on for about six weeks and now we are taking heat from the school administration due to the crowds outside the Hall and the impact our little side adventure is taking on cafeteria revenue. Finally we are busted. On a snowy Friday afternoon, while we are wrapping up, two suits walk over and ask to see our license, what license?

With a stern reply comes, "Your mercantile and your board of health for starters."

Looking at each other, we shrug our shoulders and say, "Well, we didn't know we needed any, we were just part of the anti-war demonstrations and this was our last day here."

"Good to hear," the agent says, "and don't return either, or we'll have to write you a citation and you'll have to appear in court."

"Thanks for the warning, we won't be back."

We laugh on our way back to class, shaking our heads while acknowledging we made over $4,000 each after expenses. Not bad for six weeks, working two hours a day. But nothing lasts forever, one door closes, another one opens.

While waiting for the next financial opportunity to present itself, study is the pressing issue; we missed a lot of classes during the sandwich operation. Soon the Christmas break will be here, along with mid-term exams. I need to do well to keep my parents happy, after all they are making financial sacrifices to keep me in college.

Donna is in her senior year at West Catholic Girls High and her prom and graduation will be here before I know it, need to focus. We are far more serious about our relationship than our parents realize and making plans for our future in the midst of everything going on around us.

Fall semester grades are out, and I didn't far as well as I would have liked, and my professors are disappointed in my performance. I passed all my courses but not to the level expected. I need to take my spring semester more seriously. But for now, I need to make more money for the holidays. It has always been my responsibility to put up outdoor Christmas lights for my parents, so that's first on my agenda. Our next-door neighbor is the owner of Philadelphia's famous Pat's Steak. Harry is his name; he comes out and asks if I would put his lights up, too. Of course I said yes,

Harry was always nice to me giving me odd jobs and over paying for the work.

"You should offer your services to all the homeowners in the area; this is an affluent neighborhood with most being business owners and have more money than time," he says. FLASH! Another money-making opportunity. Call Ralph, print flyers, and get supplies. Ralph is a wiz at electrical work, and I have organizational skills.

Well, to make a long story short, we distribute flyers in a ten-city block area to start. The phone begins to ring off the wall, it's constant and my mom becomes our booking agent.

Ralph and I are working twelve to fourteen hours a day, seven days a week, our offer is simple, we charge by the window and door, first and second floor all priced ala cart. Our price includes install and take down, we offer an additional charge for bulb replacement or wire repair. Our average home front job was about $40. We were making thousands of dollars a week and creating a new business with growing repeat customers to come, year after year. Not to belabor the venture at this time, my mom would call me around the holidays years afterward telling me people were asking if we were doing Christmas lights.

Christmas Day arrives with a snow blizzard. Shit, I have to get to Donna's house for dinner and I have a car full of gifts for her. I know she never really got lots of presents. I am wanting to take her breath away. News is reporting that the expressway is closed and most side streets have yet to be cleared. My dad wants me to stay home, but I am determined to get to her house no matter what convoluted route I have to take; we debate for a while, and he finally agrees to let me go. It takes about two hours when it usually takes about forty minutes. When I finally get there, she is at her front door, and she can't believe I made it. I begin the multitude of round trips necessary to get over twenty gift wrapped boxes under her tree. She can't believe her eyes, and I just want to sit and watch as she unwraps each one with a smile and a kiss for me. It's her and my best Christmas ever.

As I watch the pile of crumple wrapping paper grow, my mind finally settles on what I want to do and how to get there. First, I want to increase my GPA in the next semester. Secondly, I want to schedule summer classes in order to complete my college degree earlier than the prescribed timeframe, and lastly, I want to ask Donna to marry me after she graduates, preferably in September. That's my plan and I am committed to make it come true.

January 1997, new semester in full swing. I am taking all the coarse credits I can handle. I arrange to speak with the Dean, getting clearance to take more coarse credits in the summer months and advance my completion to earn my degree.

The Dean is agreeable and offers whatever help I may need. All I need to do is get a grade of B on my current courses and he will sign off on my advance schedule. I know what I need to do and I am totally committed to the challenge.

The spring semester is drawing to a close, and my grades are well above average, and I am so physicked for exams. They are scheduled for the second week in May, not too far away. Then Donna's graduation, she is so cute and excited for her senior year to end and a new adventure to begin. She has no idea what I am planning for September, and I am getting jitters waiting for the time to get here. I haven't even told my parents yet or my brothers. I need to set the wheels in motion if my surprise is going to work.

It's going to be a tight schedule with all my summer classes and working whenever I can. Always trying to put a few more coins in the coffers for the planned engagement and celebration I know will follow.

After graduation Donna takes a job with Bell Telephone, and I am buried in study hours to accomplish my goal of advancing my class credits toward my degree in Architectural Design and Building Construction Technology. The summer months fly by, and I am poised for fall semester and more importantly asking Donna to marry me! For a nineteen-year-old guy, it's a full and stressful plate, but I am prepared, scared to death but prepared.

SEPTEMBER 9TH, 1967

It's Saturday morning, about 8:00 A.M., I am in a slight panic, today is the most important day in my life.

Billy, who is home on leave from the Air Force, looks over and asks, "You ready for this?"

He is already engaged to his girlfriend Claudia, so he has some experience with the events to occur.

Yes rolls off my lips. I have a lot to do, the jeweler opens at 1 P.M., and with the help of our neighbor Marie, Harry's daughter and a social butterfly, I was able to get a great diamond, Marquis cut, 1.6 carrot, set in white gold.

It's a thing of beauty and the most expensive thing I ever purchased, but in my mind, nothing was too much for the girl I loved and planned to marry. It's a good thing I was able to save the money from the sandwich and Christmas light ventures.

I pick up Marie, and we are off to the jewelers; I'll try to paint a mental picture for the reader because this is a typical and seemingly normal scene for Italians living in South Philly. The Jeweler is Joe Lerro, his shop is located on the third floor of a row-home a few blocks from Pat's Steaks. The Lerro family lives on the first and second floor. When you get up to the third floor, there is a double door leading into a shop full of glass showcases and shelves with every style of necklaces and watches you can imagine. The clientele is a mix of average middle-class buyers with a sprinkle of neighborhood Wise Guys.

Marie is well-known here and is immediately greeted by Joe and reaches to present me with the ring I worked so hard to buy. It's magnificent, and everyone looks over and agrees, then come the pats on the back and a flurry of congratulations and luck with my pending engagement plans that evening.

My heart is full, and my mind is a scramble of imaginary scenarios that might play out while I am popping the question of marriage later that night.

Marie senses my apprehension and says, "Let's go get a steak sandwich." When we get to Pat's, her brother is working the grill and Harry is in the back. Harry immediately comes out to greet me with well wishes and a steak sandwich. The place is mobbed as usual with a line of people out to the street. But it's a beautiful day, and the Italian Market is bustling with shoppers.

Maria calms me down and remarks that Donna is a lucky girl to have such a devoted boyfriend and I have nothing to worry about.

"It's obvious you two are in love and this is the next step she would be hoping for, just follow your heart and everything will work out."

We finish and leave for home, Marie gives me a kiss on the cheek, and heads off. I stand frozen in time contemplating my next move, then as if I were struck by lightning, I rush off to show my family the ring. My brothers are excited for me, my dad has a big smile on his face, and my mom gives me a kiss with a tear on her cheek.

IT'S SHOW TIME.

As if it were a normal Saturday night date, I pick Donna up around 7 P.M. and we head off. Our normal routine is to stop at Larry's Steak House, pick up a sandwich, and head to a drive-in-movie. To-night is no exception, I want everything to seem inconspicuous to my motives.

I don't remember what movie was on the screen, I only re-member thinking, should I ask now, wait, go get popcorn and then ask or wait. For an ultra-confident guy, I am totally off balance. Fi-nally I take a deep breath and reach into the glove compartment and take out the small felt-covered box containing the one thing that will change my life forever.

As she wondered what was happening, I look her in the eye, open the box, and ask, with a lump in my throat, "Donna, will you marry me?"

Donna begins to cry, "YES," she cries. I take the ring from its box and place it on her finger, and with a long kiss and hug, we set in motion the destiny of our young lives.

We leave the drive-in and head back to Donna's house where her sister and parents are anxiously waiting for us. This is no surprise to them, I was respectful to ask her father for his daughter's hand in marriage well in advance of this evening; the event was inevitable, but it was important to show the respect I felt he deserved. Now Jimmy, as her father insisted I call him, shook my hand and conveyed his confidence that his daughter could not have found a better match and knew I would always take care of her and make her happy. Mary, however, at that time was a more difficult nut to crack; she was stern and opinionated and used to being the control person in her family. We always clashed but always ended up in a compromise. It's not that she didn't like me, it was that she loved her daughter more, and I got that.

When we arrive, they are at the front door recognizing the glowing smile on our faces, reach out to kiss and hug us, and like the repeating action of a machinegun, run off a barrage of questions and plans that need to be made for a celebration. I am very friendly with the neighbors and they begin to show up and call over with wishes and congratulations to us, as well as to Mary and Jimmy.

It's almost midnight, and I need to leave for home. With a long kiss and hug, I let go of Donna's hand.

"See you tomorrow," say good bye to her parents and neighbors, walking to my car I look back to see her standing at the front door holding up her ring hand and waving to me as I drive off.

Arriving home I am faced with the same scene I left at Donna's. Marie is first to give me a hug even before I get to my door; she knows there are family members waiting and she doesn't want to impose, but since she was a big part of this process, she didn't want to miss my return. She smiles and walks back to her house, I can fill her in on how things went tomorrow.

Inside things are buzzing, I can hear my mom and dad talking and planning to reach out to Donna's parents to make arrangements for an engagement party. The day and night have been exhausting, and I need to get some sleep.

Its Sunday morning, Donna and I have plans to take a ride and talk about what comes next, our destination is George's Hill, it's located within the Fairmount Park System near her home and is a favorite make out spot for teenagers. There's a parking lot at the top of the hill with a small concession stand where Park Patrol Guards on horseback stop for coffee. We are oblivious to everything, and after a long discussion, we pick June 22nd, 1968 for the day of our marriage. Now we have to break the news to family and friends.

Chapter Eleven
Life Gets Serious

I am now in my junior year and taking advantage of every opportunity to advance my credit count and take part in extra credit seminars. I am aware of the necessity to finish my required courses before our planned wedding in June.

It's close to the holiday season, and everyone is preparing for the Christmas break and the conclusion of fall semester. Between morning classes, I happen to see a posting on the community bulletin board that a position has become available within one of the new University Development Departments for a student in the Architecture school for a part-time position.

My gut tells me to skip the next class and go apply for the job. It happens to be at Mitten Hall on the third floor. The door to the new Design Department has a sign posted to walk in for appointments. I take a deep breath and walk in. There is an elderly well-dressed woman standing by a receptionist, looking up she asks if I am here for the open position.

"Yes," I reply.

"That was quick," she says. "I had that notice posted just hours ago. Hello, my name is Ruth Kelly and I am the department head."

I introduce myself and tell her, "I am here to end your search; I am certain you will be pleased with my abilities."

With a smile, she points to her private office and says, "Come in."

My interview takes about forty minutes.

In closing she tells me, "The job is yours, go down to HR and you can work flexible hours to not interfere with your scheduled classes." Leaving I notice there are four other people ready to apply, sadly Mrs. Kelly informs them the position has been filled.

As the weeks go by, I am learning a great deal from Mrs. Kelly and the other two female designers already on staff. I am the only male within the department, and Ruth, as I am asked to call her, begins to have me accompany her to design meetings with many other department heads. The University has attained national recognition, and considerable state and federal funding has become available for University expansion.

Recognizing my construction and real estate background, Ruth on occasion asks my opinion and if I think what some department heads are asking for is economically achievable.

More and more I feel Ruth is putting more weight on my ability to give a realistic opinion. Things begin to advance; I am being allowed to address the questions and concerns at high level meetings directly. I ask her why neither of the other designers, who are clearly more skilled in design with advance degrees in the arts, ever attend. Ruth confides they are too flighty when it comes to meetings that involve construction changes to departments; in order to accomplish the desired improvements, my background is more beneficial.

During these meetings, I come in contact with industry leaders from both the financial and business worlds, Ruth is quick to make the introductions and assures them I am capable of handling any problems or concerns they may have as it relates to construction, layouts, or designs. Wow, I am so grateful that my department head has that much confidence in me, and I make sure not to disappoint her.

IT'S JUNE!

My mind is singularly focused on one thing and one thing only, my marriage to Donna. My junior year is complete, I am nineteen years of age with one more year to complete at Temple. I have a decent job for now, and with a little help from our families, we can make it through the coming year.

The wedding is everything we hoped for, from the mass at 9:30 A.M. through the reception and farewell kisses. The honeymoon destination is three hours' drive to the Pennsylvania Pocono Mountains, a week to rejoice and decompress. I can recall every moment of that first week of marriage, now fifty-two years later, it's as fresh in my mind now as the carnation in my tuxedo lapel those many years ago. How lucky and blessed we are knowing we made the right choices in life.

Our time to celebrate is over for now, time to prepare for our life ahead. Going back to college will require lots of discipline and stamina.

My job at the university is secure but only offers a limited number of hours, and even with Donna now working at Liberty Mutual Insurance, we need more income. We don't want to rely on our parents any more than would be essential. I may only be nineteen-years-old, but I am a man! A man who felt mature enough to get married, so it is on me to find a way to provide.

I take a job working at Sears in the evenings as a sales associate. With my class schedule, the hours working at school, and nights at Sears, we hardly see each other, except at bedtime. These are sacrifices that need to be made, but they are only temporary.

Summer passes, and we are secure in our routine; married life has it challenges, but facing issues together and solving problems is the cement in building and keeping a relationship together and strong.

Donna hates working, and I understand getting up early for her isn't her strong suite. I do my best to make her smile knowing our first Christmas together is right around the corner, it's something positive to focus on, another milestone in our life. With the holiday season behind us, we settle in for a long winter, but life has other plans for us. In February we learn that we are expecting a baby. Late August is the projected delivery time, June is my graduation, and life promises to get complicated, like they say, "What doesn't kill you makes you stronger."

It's June, and graduation is here. I am the first in the family to have a college degree, my family is so proud. Donna is flipping between smiles and cringes as the baby is getting close to its time. I am offered a full-time position at Temple and I accept, still working nightly at Sears; that will have to end soon as I need to be close for Donna and the baby.

June passes, then July, the days of August are moving quickly. My twentieth birthday comes and goes without fanfare and all attention is now focused on the main event. The birth of our child. We have close friends who live in the apartment next to ours, Pete and Peggy; they are also expecting a baby at the same time as we are. Donna and Peg are close friends having gone to high school together. We have a lot in common, and most of our free time is spent together. It makes the anticipation and the fear easier to handle as we have each other to count on when things get scary.

Peggy goes into labor first and they are blessed with a baby boy. Pete and I are closer than ever and share in the excitement, which lasts one week, then Donna goes into labor, and on August 31st, we have a miracle, a son, we name him after me, Robert Jr., but to allow him to grow with his own identity, we only call him Robbie.

Donna and I, Pete and Peggy are virtually inseparable; we have family functions together, baby doctor appointments together, and many meals together. It is the kind of friendship that creates a bond that will last a lifetime. Two more boys are born into this friendship. We now have two sons each and celebrate birthdays and family event together. This friendship has lasted a lifetime and thrives to this day.

In September of 1970, we move to a row home in nearby Clifton Heights; it needs a lot of work, but I am capable of renovating everything with my own two hands, but when I need help, my Uncle Nick is always there, he is still giving me tools and showing me how to do things, he is a perfectionist and expects the same from me.

Donna is no longer working, and income is limited. My dad makes me an offer to come work with him in real estate. After a heart to heart with Ruth at Temple, she acknowledges my need to earn more and pleasantly wishes me good luck in the future and arranges a farewell party with staff and close friends within the department. I learned a lot from her and the contacts made will help me going forward, although I don't realize it at the time.

With some modification to my dad's office, I create a private space to work on real estate and develop an interior design enterprise. I shortly learn that the skills I have in design don't pay the bills. Things aren't going as planned, and both my dad and I know this line of work isn't for me. But I am hanging on, waiting for something to change.

It's a sunny Sunday morning in November when the phone rings; it's my dad telling me about a classified add he read in the Sunday paper. He tells me the add must have been written just for me, why I ask.

He begins to read it over the phone, "*A prominent Philadelphia Bank in search of an individual experienced in drafting, construction, and real estate, call for an interview*"

My dad knew working in his office was not my calling but also knew I would not quit and disappoint him. Unknown to me, he was always looking for an opportunity that would better suit my talents. This classified add might just be that opportunity.

The following Monday morning, I am on the phone in answer to the Sunday classified. I get an appointment for Tuesday morning to meet with the Vice President of the bank's real estate department and his assistant.

I am ready and confident about the interview. The guy they are looking for in their add is me, I know it, I just have to convince them. The interview seems to go well, and by the tone of the questions, I can tell they are interested in me as well. When the meeting is over, we shake hands with my being told they will be in touch. Upon leaving I am again greeted by Ms. Kelly, an older woman and the private secretary to the Vice President, she gives me a reassuring smile telling me she will let me know as soon as they make a decision.

Patience is not one of my virtues, so true to my nature, I call into the bank's real estate office on Wednesday and Thursday to check on the status of my interview. As usual Ms. Kelly answers in a pleasant voice and tells me I will be getting a call today for a follow-up interview. My heart is racing with anticipation. The phone rings as expected, and it's Mr. Drayton the Vice President, asking me to come in Friday morning at eleven o'clock.

"I'll be there, and thanks for the call."

My wife and dad are excited for me and wish me luck on tomorrow's interview. It's Friday, and I am up at dawn, eager for the day's events to unfold. A kiss for luck and I am out the door at the bus stop and on my way to Philadelphia.

Again Ms. Kelly greets me with a smile and says Mr. Drayton and Mr. Fury are waiting for me in his office. I adjust my jacket, take a deep breath, and walk in.

"Hello, Bob, have seat," Mr. Drayton speaks first, "you are very persistent. We have given a lot of thought to your application, and after several other prospects, we would like to offer you the position on a trial basis," he lays out the scope of the job and tells me the bank is going to be expanding and there will be room for advancement if things work out.

"I am ready, sir, all I need is a little direction and I will complete whatever task they throw my way."

Mr. Fury chuckles and says, "Well, you have big shoes to fill."

I turn and reply, "Well, I saw them on the way in, they are too small, so I brought my own boots." Shaking their heads, rise to shake my hand, and tell me I start Monday at 8 A.M.

I can't wait to get home and tell my wife the great news, she will be excited for me for a number of reasons but mostly because this is the kind of work where she knows I can excel.

With my entire family now hearing of the good news, the weekend has special significance and my mom prepares a celebratory Sunday dinner. It's a good day as I hold my two-year-old son Rob, I smile at him with the promise of life getting better.

My dad puts his hand on my shoulder and says, "Good luck, try to keep a low profile, listen and learn, you are in the business world now and having to deal with people whom you may feel are not as smart as you, keep your feelings to yourself; you're young, and nobody likes a smartass kid telling them they are wrong. Let them figure that out on their own and let them take some of the credit for your showing them a better way of getting things done."

"I get it, Dad," I reply, "I'll keep that in mind." With dinner and congratulations over, we head home to settle down and prepare for the next phase of my life.

Monday morning is a bright day in many ways. I show up with a bright smile and expectations. Mr. Drayton walks me around the department and introduces me to the staff and division heads. Everyone seems friendly and willing to help with my transition.

I am given the ability to set up my floor space in whatever way I feel works for me. I am given the agenda of work priority and a few days to gather whatever I need to get the job done. Drawing from the experience of working in a similar position at Temple, I snap to the task of ordering drafting equipment and supply catalogues. Referencing my contact list of names and phone numbers from those days, I put a team together with whom I am familiar to accomplishing the projects on the list. After a week's time, I have a plan of action, presenting it to Mr. Drayton for approval. I get the go ahead to work out the details and let him know what I need to get the job done. Asking if I am free to use contractors and suppliers, I know and trust he tells me it's in my hands. However, he gives me a list of a few people who are good customers of the bank and try to use them whenever possible.

Things are moving fast. I have lots of freedom to walk about doing what I think is in the best interest of the bank, no one is keeping track of my hours or time spent outside the office. My enthusiasm catches the attention of a Senior Vice President and calls for a meeting with Mr. Drayton and myself. A proposal is thrown out for consideration; in addition to my current duties, would Mr. Drayton have a problem of my working on a new bank building from construction to wall art.

Asking if I thought I could handle that big a project, I reply, "Yes, but I have one request. Can I submit proposals from contractors I know for consideration?" After a few minutes, they tell me the contractors have to be union to avoid any negative feedback. I agree and tell them just get me the plans and I will put a package together.

My thoughts now go back to not only what I learned at Temple but what I learned back on the streets in my shoe shine days. There is a lot at stake now, and along with it lots of potential income. If I can figure out how to save the bank money and make side deals for myself, it would be a win-win and nobody would be the wiser.

My street contacts gave me the ability to get non-union shops the cards needed to satisfy the bank but cut a side deal with me for less than what the bank would pay union competition, and I could collect a fee from my contractors.

This is working out great. The bank is happy, the work is moving quickly, I am always ahead of schedule, so no one is asking any questions as to how I am getting this done. I am making far more on the side than the salary from the bank. As things progress, the bank's purchasing department head begins to complain that I am placing orders for items that traditionally went through his department. Now I know what's happening, he is no longer getting his side deals from suppliers, it's all coming to me. The bank is run by Quakers and their image is that of being squeaky clean, but I know better. The Senior Vice President sets up a competition to end the dispute. There is a pending order ready to be placed for a branch bank getting ready for a grand opening. The directive is for the head of the purchasing department and myself to gather a total proposal price for the pending order and submit it to him for a decision.

For me this is a cake walk. I can undercut any pricing by adjusting the amount of fee I would usually get to secure the lower proposal. When the bids are reviewed, there is no contest. I have the guarantee to make all future purchases of any item that goes into a branch bank or division I have on my renovation schedule, and the purchasing department would get pencils and paper clips. Needless to say, I didn't make any friends, but at this point, I didn't care, that was not my goal.

But I am getting restless and want more from the bank in the way of compensation. I am saving the bank a ton of money over what they were accustomed to spending and felt I deserved a considerable raise in salary. Approaching Mr. Drayton, I make my case. He agrees but tells me this Quaker bank doesn't give more than a ten percent annual raise to anyone, including himself, but he will make the case for me.

Several weeks pass, and no response to my request. On a Saturday morning, I am in the office getting ready for an early Monday field meeting.

Standing outside Mr. Drayton's office, I pause for a minute, entering, I look for the folder containing reports on all employees within his department. I find mine and begin to read what was in my annual employee's report. It states that I am an exceptional asset to the department and the bank in general. It further states that my accomplishments are beyond expectations, and his concern that the bank's compensation practices if applied to me would not keep pace with this employees talents. He felt he would probable not be able to keep me.

Now knowing what the answer to my request would be, I start to make plans for my exit. My plan is simple, take control of the situation, most of the suppliers and contractors with existing orders are my people, and the bank has no idea of who they are or how to reach out to them. If I take the files and give my two-week required notice, but at the same time take my two-week earned vacation, I would have total control of the projects now underway. With this dilemma now having impact on completion dates, I am sure they would reach out to me for help.

The trap is sprung, I will offer my help as a consultant for a fee of ten percent of the contract price. The bank is in a bind and has no choice but to agree. To soften the blow, I remind them that even with my fee, they will still finish each project well below what the budget allowed.

They must now realize how ridiculous their decision was. Mr. Drayton contacts me and tells me there are no hard feelings and had he been in my shoes, would probably have done the same. He also offers me several new projects if I am interested, and the bank would pay my consultant fee. I agree to work with him but only for a few projects as I have plans to open a new business. He asks if I could recommend anyone to fill my old position. I tell him I'll have a friend I went to college with, call him for an interview.

My friend gets the position and a new career begins for him, but in appreciation, I would like a small finder's fee on any deals with my contractors, but he wants to make his own deals and I just let it go. I don't need the grief but offer no help in getting him set up on any projects. You go your way, I'll go mine. Unfortunately that was the beginning of the end.

Graduation Photo Temple University with my wife and my dad

Baptism of our son Robbie with his Aunt Babe and Fr. La Luzern,
my high school mentor and friend

CHAPTER TWELVE
Closing The Circle

Summer of 1972, we are expecting our second child at any time. My choice to leave the bank was the right thing for me to do, or at least at this time it seems so.

I am working out of my dad's office again and making plans to open a design shop in Springfield, Pennsylvania and capitalize on my past experiences and contacts for success. However, the birth of our new baby is eminent, and on September 23rd, we have a new baby boy, Brian as he will be known, is a blessing to us and puts a greater sense of urgency on my ability to provide.

Opening my new store, Windows and Walls, sets me on a schedule of fourteen hours days, seven days a week, trying to make it work. Things are slow, and a feeling of despair is settling in. After two months, the only reasonable sale is a large residential floor order. I finally decide to cut my losses and close the store. My neighbor Bob offers his garage to warehouse what was in my store, along with several rolls of residential carpet. I go back to working out of my dad's office and concentrate on selling carpeting.

It is by chance one day a guy shows up at the office smoking a cigar and wearing a felt hat, hands my dad's secretary his business card. She recognizes he must be there to see me and brings back his card. He is the regional representative for the largest carpet mill in America. I come out front to greet him and usher him back to my office. He is a character of a guy with a hearty laugh and good sense of humor. We seem to hit it off right from the start. He asks if I want to grab lunch, and we head to a local sandwich shop to continue our conversation. He tells me as a rep he can't take orders from commercial buyers, he has to refer the order to a mill dealer. With a smile, he admits when he showed up at my office, he thought he was going to a larger carpet showroom and felt he was in the wrong place.

After a long conversation and a few laughs, I make him an offer. Since I have little to no overhead, I might be able to help him secure the leads he gets from his mill and cut him in on the contract. Now John was an amiable kind of guy, not pushy or showy and certainly not greedy.

It didn't take long for an answer, "Okay, Bob, that sounds like a plan, and whatever you feel is fair is fine with me." We shake on it, finish our lunch, John says he will be in touch, and we go our separate ways.

Within a few weeks, I begin to get a few leads from John, nothing major, but they pay the bills for now. I am sure as we become better acquainted, he'll feel more comfortable with our arrangement, things will get better.

I am submitting bids on other job as well, but it seems the larger jobs are being awarded to larger and well-known flooring contractors. I get the feeling I am not being taken seriously due to my age; maybe they think I have not yet paid my dues and do not deserve the opportunities which fell at my feet. However, on the other hand, I did. I was raised to believe that opportunities are never lost, they are just taken advantage of by someone else. I kept my eyes open and my mouth shut. *Let everyone underestimate you*, I thought, *then they'll not see the hammer falling when the time comes.*

Every day was becoming a push; success did not come easily. I was doing my best and spent many hours working hard, playing by the rules, and trying to gain a legitimate edge. But more times than not, my competitors would use underhanded and unethical tactics to either beat me out of a job or find a way not to pay for the jobs I did get.

I was becoming bitter and jaded. I can recall where and when I pounded my fist on a bar and proclaimed, "No more, from here on out, I will do whatever is necessary to ensure success.

I refuse to be taken advantage of ever again and swear, from now on, there will be no depth to which I will not sink to win."

SEPTEMBER 1973

A call from my good friend Pete started me on a path that I will follow all the days of my life.

"Bob," he said, "what do you know about the Freemasons?"

"Not much, Pete. I spent some time in my senior year at Temple University writing a report on the Grand Lodge of Pennsylvania's Masonic Temple at One North Broad Street in Center City, Philadelphia from an architectural point of view and picked up some knowledge on the fraternity but not much, why?" I asked.

"A friend of mine," he said, "Harry, asked if I would be interested in learning more about it and maybe applying for membership. Pete asked if I might be interested as well."

After a short pause, I replied, "Yes."

"Let's get together," he said, "and find out more."

The conversation eventually leads us to completing and submitting an application for membership in a well-known lodge in Philadelphia.

I did some research on the fraternity and was amazed at who they were and what they stood for. They are a group of men who aspire to reach a higher standard of character with a commitment toward doing whatever they could to improve and raise the level of social behavior for the betterment of all mankind. I wanted to be part of this organization and waited anxiously for a notice in the mail telling me I had been accepted for membership. When it finally arrived, I was excited beyond belief.

I was twenty-four-years-old and being welcomed into the oldest, most respected, and influential organizations in the history of the world. *What mysteries awaited,* I thought, *and what would I learn about life that I had not yet experienced.* My initiation to the Lodge arrived, and I was awe struck. I had been in the Temple building many times before, always leaving with an unfulfilled yearning as to what really happened here when the Masons were in Lodge. I was about to find out.

The more I attended, the more I desired light and knowledge about its mysteries and teachings. Everything I had heard about the fraternity from the unenlightened was turning out to be false. What I found out was how closely their teachings were in line with my Catholic faith. The Masons, although not a religious organization, will not accept an application from anyone who does not believe in a Supreme Being; their feeling is that if you do not believe, you will someday be judged by your creator for your actions here on earth. You will have no reason to fear the results of those actions or how you treat others around you. That premise alone is the basis of the Masonic Fraternity, and they take it very seriously.

Over ten million members worldwide of like-minded men each looking out for one another.

What happens in reality was the fraternity strengthened my faith in myself and mankind in general. I would later be told at a home visit by our parish priest that as a Catholic, I was not allowed to be a Mason and could be excommunicated for being one.

With all the candor I could muster, I told him, "Be careful, Father, if you are telling me to choose, I will pick my fraternity. I love my faith but had no intention of disassociating myself with my fraternity." I continued to explain, "It was the Freemasons who gave me my first big break in life by awarding me a lucrative contract, which lasted over three years and stabilized my fledgling company." I told him I could not recall any similar contract coming from the Archdioceses of Philadelphia to help me out.

"Nonetheless," he said, "why don't you join the Knights of Columbus?"

"The Knights," I responded, "were formed after a ban on joining the Freemasons was imposed by the Vatican several centuries ago over the battle in Europe over the separation of Church and State.

Why then," I asked, "would I join the second best when I already belong to the best?"

"You would give up your faith?" he asked.

"No," I replied, "only the church. God would still judge me by my actions and not my memberships. Furthermore my fraternity never asked me about my religious beliefs nor asked me to choose. Why then should I give into pressure from my church to make non-religious choices?" This conversation went on at several levels of the church and eventually resulted in a meeting with the Archbishop, all still trying to get me to join the Knights in place of the Freemasons. Finally I asked the Archbishop, "How many Masonic meetings have you attended?"

"Why, none," he replied.

"Well," I responded, "I have been to many and I can tell you there is nothing within those meetings that would be in conflict with my faith."

He pondered for a while, and finally with his hand on my shoulder, said, "I cannot condone your actions, but if you feel that strongly about the fraternity, then follow your heart," and I have ever since.

My time spent with my Lodge has ebbed and flowed many times during my lifetime. The pressures and demands of life, raising a family, and building a business have taken priority, and hard choices had to be made. I constantly recall the explanation given in response to my questioning the Right Worshipful Grand Secretary of the Grand Lodge of Pennsylvania when I asked why the marble floors in the grand hall are a checkered pattern of one-foot square black and white tiles. The answer seamed so simple, he pointed to the area in question and told me it signified the constant struggle of good and evil. I never forgot that, and in all things, I find for every good in life, there is a competing evil, which side wins out is up to you, and with the help of God and your inner strength, you choose well more times than not.

CHAPTER THIRTEEN
The Dark Years

THE PURSUIT OF POWER, MONEY, AND INFULENCE

I was on my way; I had achieved much. Success was coming in large measure, and along with it came the trappings of Capitalism, favors received, favors owed. A slippery slope of give and take, alliances made out of necessity and posturing required to be sure you were in the right place at the right time. I was determined that would be me!

Still working out of my dad's office but with the addition of a carpet warehouse in an industrial park. A friend of my dad's was able to locate a used forklift truck, and with the help of a few friends, I set up the steel shelving necessary to stock rolls of carpet for secured contracts and stock inventory.

Being born and raised in South Philly, everybody knows everybody, especially who to go to with problems that can't be solved easily through normal channels. Two doors down from my dad's office is another real estate office run by the son-in-law of the local Don. I know him well enough but never had any dealings with him in the past. One day he walks into my office and asks if I had time for lunch, strange but not bizarre.

"Sure, Ralph, what time?"

"How about now?" he asks.

"Sure, give me a minute to close up."

"Let's take my car," he says, "I am parked right out front." Ralph has a flashy Cadillac, which is no surprise, but then again so is Ralph. We head over to a well-known stomping establishment called The Saloon. It's a pleasant lunch with non-descript small talk; after a few minutes, Ralph poses a question. My father-in-law has a job coming up and asked if I knew anyone who could handle the work and be trusted. "I thought of you right away," he says.

"What's the job?"

"Well, it involves construction and it's in Atlantic City."

"Casino work?" I ask.

"No, not really," he tells me, "but the work is located all around the boardwalk area."

"What do you need me to do?"

"We need to convert entire neighborhoods of empty buildings into operating businesses in a short period of time, then dismantle them after they are appraised and move to the next city block." Ralph continues, "It would be greatly appreciated, and in the future, if I ever needed a favor, all I would have to do is ask. I wouldn't have to wait to get paid more than a week."

Stopping him I interject, "Ralph, that isn't even a concern, I know how this works. Okay, when do you need me to start and what are the specifics?"

"Well, can you meet us in Atlantic City tomorrow?"

"Sure, just give me a time and place."

It's important to remember commitments given in this world are necessary to adhere to and to keep your word. These are serious people, and a smile can turn to a smirk in a heartbeat.

Ralph greets me as I pull up to the address; his father-in-law is talking with a few guys I recognize from the neighborhood. I stand back and wait to be introduced.

As the Don finishes his conversation, he turns toward Ralph and myself and says, "HI, Bob, nice to meet you. Ralph speaks highly of you, so I know you are the right guy for this job." He walks me around and explains what needs to get done. It's straight forward and he doesn't beat around the bush, simply explains, "We are looking to sell these properties to the casino people and with an enhanced appraisal for buildings that look like operating businesses rather than empty spaces; they will be worth much more money." He need not tell me anymore, I get the plan, better not to ask too many questions, it's just a job like any other, do what is expected, get paid, and move on.

I come up with a plan to expedite the desire result. With my carpet mechanics, we bring in rolls of carpet and stretch them from floor to ceiling; this gives the appearance of existing partition walls. They bring in furniture and whatever equipment necessary to give the look of an operating business. An appraiser comes in, takes pictures, and writes a report. After a wink and a nod, we strip the building of carpet and move to the next one and start the process all over again. In one week's time, we are completing six to eight units quickly. Ralph shows up with the Don, takes a look around, gives me a smile, and walks away. Later that day, Ralph calls me to say his father-in-law is grateful and appreciates my ingenuity, let him know how much he owes me so far, he wants me to know he won't forget the help.

"No problem, Ralph, I'll get it over to your office tomorrow."

"Great," he says. "I'll have your money in the afternoon."

It all sounds harmless, and the adrenalin rush produced is like a drug addict who must feed his habit in greater quantities at an ever-increasing rate. I can tell you from experience it is a formula for drawing unsuspecting prey into a world of shady dealings, distrust, and intimidation. A world where you always win but compromise your principals more and more with each new deal. The power derived and influence obtained grows, but so does your list of enemies.

Eventually you turn to those you know can provide the protection you need to continue on this road. You do them favors, and in turn they reciprocate slowly, building a debt you can never escape or repay. Think about that, I rationalize the events by telling myself I was only doing business and had no dealings, knowledge, or desire to be part of that life. But you grow to love the association and power it brings.

After a while, I was able to get any job or be awarded any contract I wanted. My contact was through the immediate family of the Don who asked me for some help with properties he controlled and in turn he would open doors for me in the business world of my profession. Things worked out great; it was profitable and exciting.

You never know when the next opportunity might present itself. I am always ready and have the backing of external help if needed. Now John C., my mill rep, calls me with a lead for a major project in Doylestown, Pennsylvania where a total health care community is under construction, they need a ton of flooring. We set up a meeting with the project manager, Zenon, and present our proposal. We lay out for him what we can do and how fast we can get started. The flooring selected is exclusive to John's mill; anyone bidding against us has to use the same carpet. It's a major purchase and preparing my bid, with John's help, can happen quickly. I have a plan and let John know what I am thinking; he is a little taken back with my idea but thinks he can pull it off. I place a hold on all available quantities of the carpet needed and available, and the entire next scheduled production run. This move takes other bidders installation timeline out of reach, making mine the only choice that can meet the deadlines. Needless to say, I get the contract and I don't have to low ball the bid, so there is plenty of room for profit and to cut John in on the deal.

The project manager is impressed with my work and ability to think outside the box. He asks me if I might be able to handle other areas of the project, electrical, plumbing, furnishings, etc.

"Sure," I tell him, "what do you need?" The project is moving fast and the contractors on the job can't keep up and are having Union problems. I assure him I can fix that, remembering the favors promised from Ralph, I make a call. I'm given directions on who to call and get the cards I need, his people will let the local business agents know who we are.

As time passes, Zenon and I become friendlier and the work and money are getting more advanced. Zenon makes sure my checks are always at the top of the voucher list. In return he asks a favor. "Sure, what do you need?"

He begins to tell me there is a restaurant he is trying to build and open in the Queens Village section of Society Hill, Philadelphia and is running into labor problems. I know where this conversation is going and quickly stop him from going on.

"Where is it, and what's it called?" With that information, I make a few calls, and in two days, he calls to thank me, problems solved. A small price to pay for the money and work he is giving me. But I know it is the weight of yet another favor placed upon the scales of give and take.

Another call from John, his mill has a lead for a townhouse development in a well to do neighborhood just outside the city called Chestnut Hill. We set up a meeting to meet the project manager, Joe C., this guy presents himself as a slender, well-dressed high flyer, well-groomed, and his initials appear to be on everything in the room down to the cuff links on his shirt. I give John a smile, looking back at me with that WHAT? look. I know the type, it's great for me, he can be bought. We carry on a conversation with slick subtle hints and innuendoes, John has no idea what is happening, but with an unwritten agreement between Joe and myself, the contract is ours.

I now have a pre-paid stock of carpeting from John's mill in my warehouse, enough for the entire project, even the phases not under construction. It has a wholesale value of over $45,000.

Again I reach out for Ralph to arrange for the cards I need for a union job. Before long I had my own limo with several body guards licensed to carry guns, as did I, tools necessary to effectively function in this world of deceit and double cross. I had access to all union trades and whatever license or permits needed to get the advantage over any competitor.

One day while driving myself, I check in on the Chestnut Hill job; from out of nowhere, I am grabbed from behind by a Union representative on the job who thought I was trying to put *scabs* to work. I reach for my 9mm and stick it up to his neck. One of the job foremen I knew runs up to him and whispers quickly in his ear who

I am. He quickly releases his grip and rushes to shake my hand and apologize for the breach of respect. Still gasping for air, I nodded and moved away, knowing that in a few more seconds, I would have shot this asshole. I never went to another job again without my limo and armed associates.

Things are getting more involved, and it's hard to pretend it's just business as usual anymore. Out of the blue, I get a call from Zenon about a big job coming up in Center City in which he is involved, wanting to know if I had the time to meet him and check it out. It turns out I am familiar with the building where he wants to meet, it's just down the street from the Masonic Temple. I've walked by it many times on my way to lodge, but it has always been boarded up. When I get there, several others are already in the first-floor lobby of this old hotel. Zenon greets me and introduces me to another architect who I already know; he was one of my professors at Temple, never liked the man, he always came off as better than others. He says hello and reminds me that while I was working with Ruth Kelly and renovating the old architecture department, I put his office in the lower level with no windows.

"Nothing personal," I said, "it had to be someone's office, and I guess you drew the short straw." There are other men talking in the distance who I did not know. Shortly we are all in one group, they tell me this building, which they just purchased, was on the list of acquisitions necessary to complete a new government project to connect Suburban Station Concourse with other commuter railways. The government wants an appraisal for the purchase and they need to make some cosmetic changes to get a better value as an operating hotel rather than a vacant building. Sounds familiar!

"I know what you want, who is in charge of this project?"

"I am," says a stocky older guy, Harry K. is his name and he is one of the principal attorneys in a prominent law firm here in town. One of the other attorneys in the firm happens to hold a federal position within the department of transportation in DC. I just play naïve and go along with the program, like my dad always said, become a lawyer, it's a license to steal.

The program is simple, they want the first four floors of this old hotel to look like they are fully functional suites, and my job is to make them look that way as quickly as possible. Now these guys work in a quasi-legitimate arena, not at all part of my street connected world. But relying on my past experiences with Zenon, I agree to do the work.

Now the high rise next to this hotel will definitely be affected during the demolition, and while I am working there, the owner of that office building comes over to ask questions. He is also an attorney but a younger guy named Steward. Nice guy, and we begin to meet on a regular basis. He tells me he is interested in renovating his building also and would like me to give him quotes on new carpeting. Stewart and I become friends and I make him a proposition.

"I'll show you how to save money if you show me how to keep mine." We work well together and spend business and social time together.

The contract with the hotel investors calls for a cheap grade of carpeting, John C. to the rescue, his mill has just cut a color from one of their commercial carpet lines and have an abundance of that color in stock, it's called Grey Valid; they have about 2,000 square yards they want to dump. If I buy it all, I can get it for $0.75 cents a square yard. I can easily sell it for $2.50 a square yard and I have two large jobs to use a lot of it at one time.

My job at the hotel is now done, and the appraisal is complete. Now I never was the kind of guy who counted the nickels in someone else's pocket. I just want what is due me. The balance the hotel investors owe me is substantial, and several months pass without being paid. Mr. K. keeps assuring me I will get paid soon. It's now ninety days past due, and John's mill is pressing for payment. My first invoice is $30,000, and I was getting the bums rush and stall tactics. I was not amused, the pressure from the carpet mill for payment on their invoice is constant now. I could have gone broke and lost everything if forced to take that big a loss. Despite being told my check was coming, it never did.

Not sure what to do, I consult with my friend Stewart for legal advice. Stewart knows Mr. K.'s reputation and he tells me trying to collect would cost me more in legal fees than what he owes me and I probably would still not get paid.

"Thanks anyway, I'll handle it my way."

He covers his ears and says, "Don't tell me any more I can't defend you if I know what you did." He wasn't being funny, he was serious and knew of my connections.

Again I need a favor and I know who to call, my usual contact says, "I'll get back to you." I receive a call and instructed to go to a little bar on a small street in Center City at eight o'clock the next morning. There I would be met by two loyal and persuasive associates, Al and Freddie, who had colorful street names (not mentioned here), yet were truly scary characters. Their hands engulfing mine in a handshake as they introduced themselves. They told me their instructions were to do whatever I needed to get the desired result. I explained the situation and the amount owed.

"Fine," Al said, "we'll add $5,000 for our side and you keep the balance." I give them the location of Mr. K.'s office, which is only a few blocks away and on the thirteenthth floor.

The plan was simple, they would convince him to pay me in cash and we would go our separate ways, or he would go a separate way on his own. This was now serious shit, and I was now neck deep in the world I told myself I was not a part of but merely a perimeter participant, it was all crashing down on me now, but there was no going back.

All these thoughts were going through my mind as we walked toward the office building where a life-changing event was about to take place. We looked like a walking goalpost with Al on one side and Freddie on the other. I appeared to be the short cross bar by comparison.

As we stepped off the elevator, we are greeted by the receptionist, "Good morning, Mr. Ciampitti," she says, "is Mr. K. expecting you?" No, I replied and was told Mr. K. could not see us, we would need an appointment.

Al smirked and said, "Bob, where is his office?" I pointed it out, and Al told the receptionist don't worry, he was sure it would be fine, and we walked into his private office where an obviously annoyed Mr. K quickly hung up the phone and asked what the hell I was doing there. "He's here to collect what you owe him," Al said. Freddie closed the office door and stood guard to insure there would be no interruptions. Al walked over and removed a chrome plated instrument of persuasion from his jacket assuring him this was no joke. Mr. K. was told to write a check for $35,000 to cash, he was to call the bank manager on the first floor and instruct him to cash the check and put the money in my briefcase. Al assured him that the check or the contents of his skull would be on the desk if he did not comply. He wrote the check, made the call, and I went down to collect the money. I was to call and let them know when I got back to the bar, they would then leave this asshole's office, who's shorts by then would be surely soiled, then meet up with me to split the money.

Thank God all went as planned; I was never so scared in my life. I had other experiences along the way but none this serious. I was getting in too deep and knew it. This was exactly how my dad explained guys get involved, and if you were not careful, they would eventually own you.

I received several calls from Mr. K. apologizing for the delay in payment and assured me he had every intention of paying me and that it was all just a misunderstanding.

This guy was so hated in the business community due to his arrogant attitude and business practices of shorting or not paying vendors. Word spread quickly as to what happened, and I became the toast of the town so to speak.

I started to receive many calls from people who wanted to do business with the guy who put Mr. K. in his place. So much work that I had to expand my operation and hire more people to keep up with demand.

It was a great time, and no one screwed with me from then on, the power was going to my head and things were getting heavy. My family had no idea what I did for a living or who I was working with. My mother would tell me she would have dreams that keep her up and wanted to know if I was involved with a certain element of people. I knew what she was asking and assured her I was not. I didn't like lying to my mother, but I saw no reason to make her worry.

From the outside, there is a sense of glamour to this life, but I assure you unless you are able to disconnect yourself from your emotions and moral compass, the stress of staying at the tip of the spear takes a toll on your ability to take time to evaluate confrontational situations and just immediately jump to the easy solution.

On one occasion, John and I are sitting with an architect who is working on specifications for a new hotel in Center City. We are making a presentation and getting no sense of courtesy from this guy, he is just looking over some papers on his desk and nodding his head.

I stop short and ask, "Do you have any questions?"

He finally looks up and calls out to an older woman sitting behind us with, "Mom, these guys are trying to take advantage of me, what do you think?"

She replies, "Get rid of them you don't have to do business with them."

Like the pressure plate of a land mine going off, I jump up and turn to her and say, "Piss off, bitch, we're not talking to you," then quickly turn to face this guy, "Listen, asshole, I am done being polite, this is not a debate, here's my card, there is a number on the back. I suggest you call it; if we don't get the job, you don't build the hotel." The guy is obviously stunned and says nothing. John is also stunned and gets up with us and we walk out.

Now I never heard for sure whether he called the number or not, but a week later, we get a signed contract for the hotel carpeting. At this point, my presentations for a contract is more like telling than asking. My reputation has now spread throughout the industry, so in most cases, it's a short presentation. But even with the connections at my disposal, my contracts are fair and competitive, I just don't have time for the dance. I have several installation crews working seven days a week both Union and non-Union, no time for bullshit.

My brother Bruce is now working for me in the warehouse developing the residential portion of the carpet business. I never had time for that, but since he and a crew are there seven days cutting and loading our installation vans each night for the next day's work, it's an easy addition for him.

At one point, we thought of adding a large new sign outside our building, but weeks of delays in fabrication cause me to re-think the order and call to cancel. I get a call back from the sign company that there is no refund.

I ask, "Is the sign done?"

"No," he responds. Then why no refund? I don't like his answer. I tell my head foremen Johnny to call him every day, and since his shop is only a few blocks away, stop by and push him.

The owner not liking my harassment decides to send a Union shop steward around to question my workers and truck drivers. My foreman Jonny warns him to back off for his own good. The jerk doesn't heed the warning and continues. I have no freaking patience for this shit and place a call to Ralph. He tells me to set up a meeting with this asshole at my office at nine o'clock. Johnny makes the call and thinking he has finally rattled me agrees to come.

The next morning, Ralph and two other guys show up early and are waiting with me in my private office. Jonny is out front waiting for the business agent. When he shows, he is told to go in, they are waiting for you. He walks in with a shit-eating grin on his face, he stops cold, and Ralph tells him to sit down. With a little help, he is pushed into a chair and Ralph makes a call; here is the dialogue.

"Yeah, he is here now, okay." Ralph hands this guy the phone and says, "It's for you."

Nothing comes from his mouth except, "Sorry, I didn't know." Ralph takes the phone from his hand and tells him to get out. You could almost smell the fear as he leaves the office. Johnny follows him out to the parking lot when he turns to Johnny and says, "You put me in the room with the Mafia!"

Johnny smiles and says, "I warned you, why didn't you listen?" then turns and walks back inside.

That afternoon the sign guy returns my deposit.

"Thanks," I tell him, "but I expect a new sign next week. The new sign looks good," I tell my brother. This life is making me sick, and I know I need a change.

My doctor puts me on Valium and tells me, "Death is nature's way of telling you to slow down." I decide to sell the business to my brother and do something else.

CHAPTER FOURTEEN
A New Beginning

SPRING 1976

I left Philadelphia and headed for the less metropolis streets of the Jersey Sea Shore. There I set up a construction company, bought forty building lots along with my dad and Zenon, who acted as the architect and construction designer for a totally new type of building panelizatioin with a lumber company in Baltimore, Maryland.

Several general contractors in the area had complained to the local building inspector that we were employing unfair practices and they were not able to compete. After a review of the sealed plans, it was determined we were complying with all necessary building codes and perfectly legal.

With that we were off and running; this new system allowed us to put five two story duplex homes under roof in a week's time. I handled the construction side; my dad and brother were covering the marketing and sales, and Zenon would stop by once a week to see how things were going.

By fall of 1979, we had completed and sold all the units we could build and dissolved the company. I was now looking for a new challenge. I was spending most of my time at the shore traveling back and forth to my family home in Delaware County, Pennsylvania.

My dad had a long history with Wildwood Crest, New Jersey having traveled there right after the war and along with my mom purchased a small summer cottage. He began buying up adjacent building lots and working with a local builder, mentioned in a previous chapter, became his land bank.

Let me digress for a moment; in 1955 my dad, along with forty partners, purchased at a tax sale a large section of the island, known as Diamond Beach, it was directly adjacent to Wildwood Crest but located in Lower Township. It ran from the beach to the bay and from Wildwood Crest to the Coast Guard Base. All in all, it was about 140 acres. Unfortunately from 1955 to 1969, they were only able to get two parcels near the beach developed.

By now the partnership had dwindled down to only six remaining partners, and they, too, were tired of the constant delays. Along with one of my close contractors, we made a proposal to purchase a group of forty-eight building lots, which we undeveloped and to date inaccessible, my partner Harry had the equipment and skill to bring in dozers and cut in rough streets. We set up a table in the middle of the road with maps and lot numbers, we put an ad in the local paper, and in one sunny weekend, we sold out every lot.

One year later, I purchased an additional sixty lots from my dad's group and sold them in about six months. I now had a movement and made beneficial connections with township and county officials who were friendly and willing and able to help me develop the raw ground.

In the past, my dad and his group were considered outsiders, and the members of the township planning and zoning boards resented them. Whenever there was a meeting scheduled, it was always on the second Thursday of the month, and they seemed to always be at the bottom of the agenda. After waiting for hours to be called inevitably they would be told the board is ending their deliberations for the evening and the remaining applicants would have to re-schedule. My dad usually had me tag along to see how things were done, but on the ride back home, my dad always looked despondent at not having accomplished anything. That look stuck in my mind for years.

In 1979 a deal was put together with another local developer, Tommy D., who was interested in buying a large portion of Diamond Beach from me, if I could get the local approvals needed to improve the land. Putting together a proposal with the help of my dad and accountant, it was presented to the five members of his group. It was a large purchase, $3,350,000. Knowing a deal could of been put together with Tommy D. and cover the purchase, I was confident. My dad was skeptical as he did not know the full particulars of my side deal with Tommy, and I could not tell him as he was the General Partner in the group and would have a fiduciary responsibility to tell the group all the details. I knew if they had that knowledge, they would cut a deal with Tommy directly and I would lose the opportunity. So to keep my dad on the right side of his obligations, I kept the information from him until after the deal was signed.

In order to make this whole transaction work, I had to close on the purchase with the group first, have the title company leave the closing open, and then close with Tommy in order to have the funds to pay the group. The title company went along with the timing and the transaction went off without a hitch. In return for the title agent's help, I placed all my sales through his office from that day until he retired years later. It was a great relationship through all that time.

Now I was standing in my dad's shoes with the township zoning and planning boards. My dad suggested a meeting with the township council and both boards at a scheduled work session held once a month at the municipal building. I did as my dad suggested but don't think he was prepared for my presentation.

The meeting opens as usual and the agenda is read; as usual we're the last entry on the agenda. Locating the guy on the agenda ahead of me, I ask to see him in the outside hallway.

I make him an offer, "Listen, I have a long way back to Pennsylvania tonight and don't believe the council will have enough time to call me. Knowing they'll call you because you are local, when they do, if you will tell them you are willing to give your time to me and reschedule your presentation for next month, I'll give you $1,000." He looks shocked; a thousand dollars to a local is a month's pay.

He asks, "For real?"

"Real as a heart attack." He agrees.

When the council secretary calls his name, he does as we discussed; the council members are stunned and ask, "Are you sure?"

"Yes," he replies. They look at each other in confusion. I automatically walk up to the microphone and introduce myself. They are not sure what to do, but they proceed anyway. I tell them I am the new owner of the Diamond Beach parcel and I am planning to develop it immediately.

The chairmen retorts, "Well, you'll have to get approval from us to proceed." I tell them I am planning to stay within the zoning criteria, and as a by-right plan, they have no choice but to approve my plan or pay me for the value of the property.

I continue with, "I have been here on many occasions with my dad before only to watch his efforts be dismissed, tabled, or rejected, **MAKE NO MISTAKE, I AM NOT MY FATHER, HE IS A GENTLEMEN, AND YOU TOOK ADVANGAGE!** I intend to build with or without your approval; if you try to stop me, I will sue you. I have the time and money to win."

My dad is in shock. The council chairman stands and in a loud voice tells me he resents that I am trying to turn his meeting into a circus.

With the typical arrogant, cocky attitude developed on the streets, I respond, "Well, with seven clowns on the board, it isn't hard to do," turn and walk out, meeting the postponed applicant in the parking lot, handed him $1,000 in cash, get in my car with my dad, and leave.

My dad and I don't say much on the ride home, I know this is not his style, but I look at him and say, "Well, like Al Capone once said, 'You get a lot more done with a handshake and a gun than just a handshake.'" He doesn't smile, just shakes his head and tells me I should try not being so arrogant.

"You attract more bees with honey than salt."

I smile and say, "How's that working for you, Dad? We're in a whole new world now, Dad, your word is not your bond and a hand shake can't be trusted anymore. Julius Caesar once said, 'The guy with the gold makes the rules.'"

As I drop him off, he turns and says, "Maybe you're right, good night, talk to you tomorrow."

Next day Ralph calls asking how I'm doing and what was going on with me. He tells me my name came up at a meeting with his father-in-law and some of the guys I worked with in Atlantic City, asking how I was. I told him I purchased the Diamond Beach Property from my dad and his partners, needed a change, so I sold my carpet business to my brother Bruce. There was so much to do at the shore, it needs my focus to get that project off the ground but having issues with the local government.

Silence on the other end and then, "Let me call you back in a few minutes."

Shortly after we hang up, Ralph calls back. He asks when I will be at the shore again.

"I can be there tomorrow if you need me."

"Can you meet us tomorrow?"

"Us?" I ask.

"My father-in-law and I would like to introduce you to someone who can help you."

My ears perk up, "No problem, where and when?"

He gives me an address and says, "How about noon?"

"I'll be there."

It wasn't long before my past would catch up with me. I was introduced to a local retired businessman from New York who was part of the biggest "FAMILY" there, who now lived in Wildwood Crest and was asked by the Don to look out for me. His name was Charlie and he was well-known. Everyone knew who he was and showed him the respect he had earned. If you had a problem that seemingly couldn't be solved, you went to see him, and if you traveled in the right circles, the problem was taken care of. Charlie introduces me to his group, and before long I was considered to be his protégé and treated accordingly.

On the first Thursday of every month, there was a dinner sponsored by Charlie and attended by well-connected individuals from

Philadelphia, New Jersey, New York, and Italy at a restaurant in the center of Wildwood. It was known as the Gourmet Club. There would be anywhere from sixty to 100 guys there engaged in a variety of conversations and problem-solving discussions for hours. Charlie always introduced me as Don Roberto, and to tell the truth, it made me a little nervous, but Charlie assured me it was a sign of respect he felt I had earned.

He introduced me to those he thought could open doors but cautioned others to say away. He told them I was a hard-working businessman and not a street operator. I had already been there and done that. I was a new member from Philadelphia who the Don asked to guide and help with local problems. Charlie did just that. The first power player I met was an attorney and the solicitor for the township where my property was located and could do a lot to help me with issues.

It didn't take long for the word to spread that I was Charlie's fair-haired boy, and everything got a little easier. Doors had opened that had previously been closed, and in some cases, closed and locked. I loved the way the "do me this service and someday I will return the favor" works. It is a beautiful concept of give and take and more effective than anything I have come across in life thus far. Hard work was the key, but with a little help from Charlie, I quickly grew and prospered.

It's time to stake my claim and set the stage for how I will be conducting my development business in Diamond Beach.

Beginning with the construction of several commercial buildings along Pacific Avenue, which is the main drag on the island. The center building is where my offices are located, they are on the second floor. They are protected by closed circuit TV cameras and electronically controlled access entrances. No one entered unless first cleared by myself or my secretary. There is a second concealed exit at my disposal, should the need occur. That door was also monitored 24/7.

Determined to send a clear message, in the parking lot there were three thirty-foot flag poles, the center had the American Flag, on one side it's flanked by the original continental patriot's flag showing a segmented snake with the moto "Don't Tread On Me," the other side flew the skull and crossbones. Subtilty was not one of my virtues.

Some found it offensive, some humorous, and some knew the meaning. In any event, no one rang the doorbell who wasn't invited.

During this time, road work and ground clearing was underway behind my office building. That property had laid vacant since before World War II; on the property there were a series of telephone poles, which stretched from the main bridge accessing the island, several miles away and lead to the secure Coast Guard Loran Base, across from my building and running along the Atlantic Ocean. Despite my arrogance, I felt it prudent to contact the base commander regarding the removal of the poles.

Sending a letter of concern, I received a response advising that those poles were obsolete and we had permission to dismantle them as we saw fit. With that confirmation in hand, I instructed my dozer operator to cut them down. He asked if he could salvage and keep all the copper within the cables.

"Sure," I told him, and with that, the cutting began.

Within one hour from when the cutting began, my secretary runs into my office and tells me to come to the rear window, SHIT! What the hell is going on now? I can see a black helicopter on the ground next to the bulldozer, my operator is standing with his hands in the air, and there are two armed soldiers also dressed in black standing with him.

Grabbing my jacket, I rush out to address the volatile situation with the letter from the base commander in hand.

"What's the problem?" I ask after explaining I am the land owner and this man worked for me.

I am apprised of the situation and told the base commander is on his way over as well. Apparently these poles are not obsolete, and by cutting them, communications between the Loran over the horizon radar at the base and Washington DC have gone out. That is what prompted the emergency appearance of the military.

When the commander arrives, he confirms his permission to dismantle the lines, and my operator, who is in his seventies and severely shaken, is told he can put his hands down and leave.

It seems in the early 1960's, updated communication lines were to be installed for these essential communications along the renovated Pacific Avenue. It seems that never happened and the base commander was never advised that the old lines were still in use.

That whole event did not go un-noticed by the locals, and it only made my presence on the island more noticeable and the topic of many dinner table conversations. It also did not go without notice to the township officials either. But due to an obviously embarrassing situation, the details of the event were never articulated, so it appeared to many. I had a higher level of contacts. I let it stay that way, it played to my advantage.

CHAPTER FIFTEEN
The Danger Of Power And Connection

My dad would always say when you throw a stone in a lake, the circle starts out small, but if you watch it closely, you can see how the circles expand ever outward from the original impact.

That principal can be applied to may circumstances and mine were no exception. One of those circles caught the attention of another New York family. At a Gourmet Club dinner, I am introduced to two brothers, Joe and Sal; they are connected with an influential well-known family. They are friendly with Charlie and the Philadelphia family. In a casual conversation during dinner, they tell me they are building two night clubs in the Cherry Hill area of New Jersey.

They continue with, "You are highly recommended as the guy to go to for getting things done, we should meet next week and work something out."

It turned out these clubs were seriously behind schedule, and they needed someone to pull the finishing touches together. Fortunately I have crews who are now accustomed to this kind of push and able to get the first club finished in time for the scheduled grand opening. The second club was less critical, so getting that completed would be less of a problem.

At the grand opening, Joe gives me a VIP pass, and when my wife and I pull into the parking lot, the line is around the building. We are quickly greeted and escorted through the line and taken to the center of the main dining room. Waiters carry a table and chairs quickly to our location, china, glasses, and flowers are immediately placed on the white table cloth. In a few minutes, Joe and Sal come over to say hello and greet my wife with a bottle of champagne.

"Everything is on us, Bob, enjoy the meal and show."

Donna is surprised and asks, "What's this all about?" I tell her it's just appreciation for my helping get the club open in time. It's a glamorous scene. By now the word has spread to the general public as to who the owners are, and that attracts more inquisitive patronage, it's good for the club. With the attention we are getting, the surrounding tables must feel we are part of that world; we are not, but it still plays into your psyche.

As we have all heard many times, nothing in life is free and everything and everyone has a price. You just need to figure out what buttons to push to get the reaction you need. If you do not believe this premise to be so, you are kidding yourself. Life is a beautiful thing and truly a gift from our creator, but life comes with trials and hurdles, which need to be navigated if we are to grow. That holds true for both our physical and spiritual well-being. If we are not careful, we can convince ourselves that by exceeding in one area, we can ignore the other. More times than not when we succeed in our worldly endeavors, we don't feel the need for spirituality.

That is exactly what was happening. As my notoriety grew, so did my arrogance and drive for more and more power and influence. I drifted further from reality, living and spending more time in this alternative world, walking down a different path, and this path was set to a fast pace. It had a few warning signs along the way and no shoulder to pull off if you had trouble. The only rule was to keep moving and ignore any regrets.

There were numerous rewards to this life style but little peace. It was the equivalent to sleeping with one eye open at all times; there is sleep but no rest. That was the trade-off, but at the time, it was a price I was willing to pay. Now it was payback time for the wrongs I had to endure when I was trying to play by the rules. Rules are for suckers, and I had long since left abiding by rules behind.

The exception was my family. My wife and children were then and always my first priority. My boys were getting older and needed me now more than they needed their mother. The skills they would need in life to survive with street smarts would have to come from me, and I made sure I was where I was supposed to be when it came to them. There were some tradeoffs I was no longer willing to make. I slowly began to refocus on what I wanted for my family; values, principals, and ideals were at the top of the list and it would be me having to show them the way, I possessing them once myself but traded them away a long time ago. I desperately wanted them for my children, the time was coming when I would have to make hard but obvious choices. I knew it would not be easy getting away from the contacts I made and the obligations I had yet to repay.

I was thirty-two-years-old; it was 1980 and I had it all, money, cars, property, and power. Everywhere we went, we had company; it carried over to my personal life as well. Whatever we wanted we could get, reservations, tickets, front row all the way. When everyone else was told no, not possible, sorry, we were welcomed and told yes, no problem. Whenever my wife would ask how was this always possible, I would tell her it was a show of appreciation and respect for favors I was able to do or able to get done. It was just a way of saying thank you. I don't know if she believed me or not, but she never questioned me about the details. I made sure there was never anything too far out of the realm of what would seem normal, so no suspicions were raised.

But things were about to take a sharp, serious, and dark turn, one that I was not prepared for or saw coming. In March of that year, a war broke out in Philadelphia between rival factions of the family, beginning with the assassination of the Don. All hell broke loose and things were out of control. Over a short period of time, almost everyone I had met or knew were gone, shot, killed, or in hiding in survival mode.

I was a non-combatant, and no one was watching me or what I was doing. I had only business dealings with a select few, and they were gone. I always knew the arena I was in and not as innocent as it appeared, but I just had a selective memory. One thing was now clear, if I was going to be given an opportunity to get out and turn my life around, it would be now. Once in you don't just quit or take a leave of absence. The Mafia is NOT an equal opportunity employer.

Angelo Bruno with Phil Testa

Bruno killed

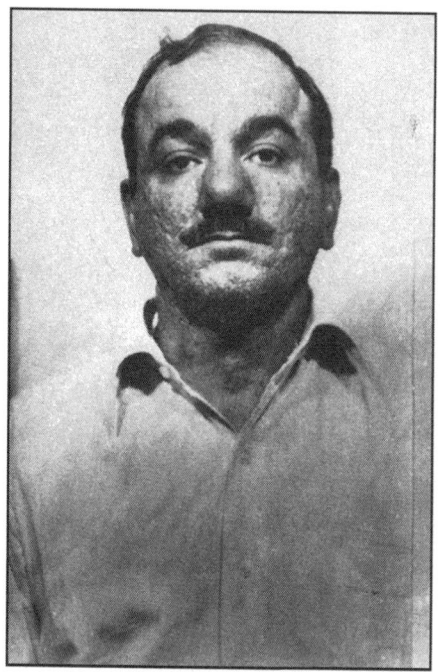

Testa Mug Shot

Testa Assassination

Narducci walking to court

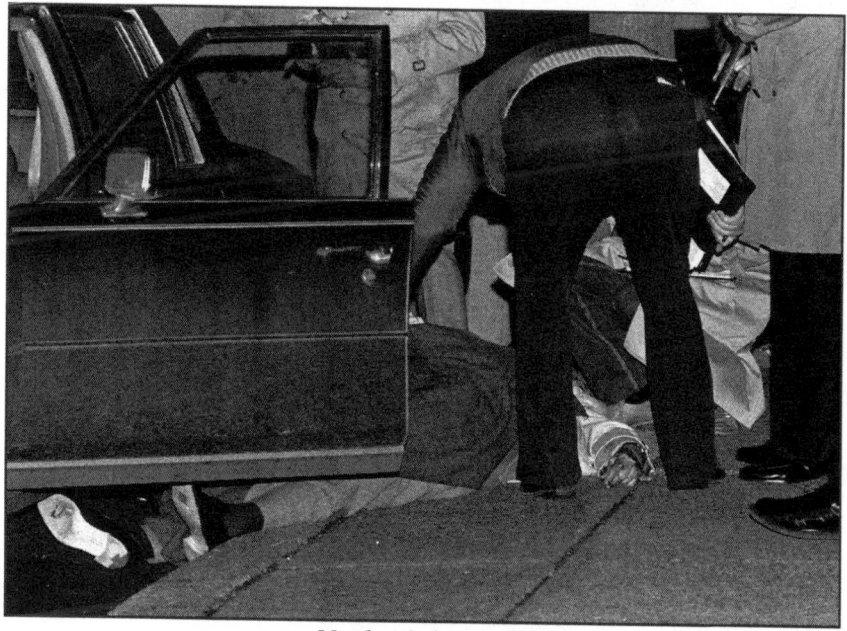

Narducci shot dead

I would take neither the high or the low road but something in-between, it was not yet clear which!

I had spent the last ten years making contacts and establishing relationships on many levels. I no longer needed to prove myself, my reputation was known and alliances fixed. There was also a list of those who would have liked to see me in jail, but I was protected. Now they thought I might not be, and this was an opportune time to make a move. I guess they thought I was without the muscle I once had. They were wrong!

The one thing I learned from the streets was that most assassins come to you with an olive branch in one hand and a dagger in the other. It didn't take long. I received a call from an attorney who was campaign manager for the mayoral candidate in a municipality where I had a large real estate investment. He represented the political party opposite mine and wanted to meet with me to discuss a possible partnership. I knew this guy and had dealt with him many times in the past; he was never on my side, always trying to work against me. In short he was a total asshole.

At this point in my life, all business was conducted out of my limo. I had it custom made to suite my purpose and it added to my security. If he wanted to talk, it was the only place I would meet him. I am suspicious but agree to meet him and set up a time.

Two days before the meeting, I receive a call from another attorney who I consider a friend. He was also the previous solicitor of the same municipality and in line for an appointment as a judge. He gives me a cryptic message that went something like this:

You are going to be set up. The guy who calls you for a meeting will be wearing a wire, he will ask you to donate a large amount of money in cash to his candidates campaign, the amount asked for would be illegal; in exchange for that donation, I will be promised favorable treatment in my land deals when his guy is elected. They want you out of the picture, he told me, whatever you do, don't agree to anything, just tell them you would be happy to donate the legal amount, but it would have to be by check.

The meeting went exactly as he described, and I responded exactly as my informant outlined. The plot was confirmed several times by people I knew and respected. With or without my long-time associates, I already had a book of favors given and favors owed, happy to see some guys were still looking out for me as well. If nothing else, I prided myself on being a man of his word and would finish and play whatever hand I was dealt.

I could see even at that point, it was going to take some time to find my way back to the peace and comfort I once knew, but it was where I wanted to be and was determined to get there.

I was fighting many battles at that period in my life, secular battles, among my adversaries were notably the US government, the Army Corp of Engineers, Fish and Wildlife. and the New Jersey Department of Environmental Protection. It was a stressful time. and I was not accustomed to losing. I dug in and fought the good fight. The facts and truth were on my side but eventually realized it was a battle I could not win, nor would they let me win. There was too much at stake. I was known but not liked by these people, and they would do anything not to be embarrassed in case law.

They had unlimited resources and the ability to change the rules whenever they fell behind in testimony, plus they had a federal judge to rule in their favor whenever they couldn't win on their own merits.

I still had not yet learned to control my anger and arrogance, being bull headed with a screw you mentality, which worked well when I had the protection of my street associates, but would not serve me well now, this was the federal government.

I did it anyway, decided if I was going to lose, don't give them the satisfaction without a fight. It turned into a real pissing contest with the judge, the US Attorney's office, and my attorney, who did his best to keep things in balance. I wasn't having it; every time they hit me, I hit back, it became a verbal blood bath every day.

The judge and I developed an open hostility toward each other and at times it would spill out in open court. On one occasion, while court was in session, the judge cautioned me about not employing any intimidation tactics on members of the Corps if confronting them on field inspections. My attorney objected, only to be rebuked.

After he gaveled to close, I confronted the judge as he left the bench and said, "Your honor, if I was who you thought I was, you would not have made it to court today," turned and walked away. The next day while sitting in the courtroom waiting for this jerk, I decided to make a statement of disrespect. When the bailiff declares all rise, I remained seated. Seeing me sitting there, the judge walked out without ever dropping the gavel. In a few minutes, the bailiff returns and tells my attorney the judge wants to see him in chambers.

When he returns, he tells me what happened as we leave the courtroom and stand in the hallway.

While there the bailiff comes over and addresses me with, "The judge is annoyed at your behavior in court, you are supposed to stand when a judge walks into the courtroom."

"Is that the law?" I asks.

"Not really, it's a sign of respect."

"Well," I say, "there in lies the conundrum, I don't respect him, he's not God, just an old man in a black robe, he wasn't elected, he was appointed; people like me pay his salary. I pay three professionals big money to show up with me every day we are here, screw him, he should stand up when I walk in the room." Dead silence! Snarling at him, I turn, grab my briefcase, and leave.

The following appearances aren't any better; one day being cross examined by a female assistant US attorney who is asking questions in a manner I find confrontational, my responses were answered in a flip manner. The judge, sensing the rise in tension, calls for a fifteen-minute recess.

In the hallway while talking to my attorney, she comes over in a huff and in my face says, "Maybe you wouldn't think it's a joke if we have the IRS look into your tax returns."

I take a step closer, almost standing on her feet, and tell her, "Maybe you should look under your hood before you start your car."

"Is that a threat?"

"No," I say, "I'm Italian, that's a promise." My attorney attempts to break up the confrontation, but I quickly add, "In the words of Al Capone talking to Elliott Ness on the steps of the federal court house, 'You fuck with me and I'll fuck with you.'" Her boss, the US Attorney, rushes over and breaks up the conversation; he must have reported the incident to the judge because he returns and calls over to my attorney, telling him court is adjourned for today and wants to see them both in chambers.

This pissing contest went on for over three years, each side taking advantage of any situation to rile the other. There is one incident that still remains fresh in my mind as if it were yesterday.

Meeting with my attorney in advance of trial for coffee at a sandwich shop next to the Federal Court House, he receives a call from the judge's chambers. Our scheduled court time is being bumped due to an emergency trial ahead of us. When we get to the court room, we are admitted to sit in the gallery to watch what is going on with the emergency trial.

At the defendants table sits a contingent of four members of what appears to be an organized crime family from north Jersey, alongside there is an equal number of female members who are either wives or significant others watching and listening un-attentively at the proceedings, while the prosecuting attorney, who is a female, is going over a transcript of tape recordings from wire-taps of the defendants. At one point, she makes mention of a conversation where one of the defendants was being told that someone was not cooperating with his instructions. The response seemed to be, well, if he won't listen, just whack him! The defendant is asked what exactly he meant by that comment. With a sarcastic attitude, he responds that it is a term used to mean screw him, we just won't do business with him.

Now neither myself or my attorney can't believe what we are hearing because even if you only watched episodes of *The Un-Touchable*, you know what that term means. However, in this case, it seems to be an acceptable explanation.

Back at the female table, one woman is eating a hoagie, another is eating pistachios and throwing the shells on the floor. How could this be going on without repercussions? I guess there must be a sense of real concern about who these people are, me they want to throw in jail for filling a few acres of wetlands. What bullshit this is? I develop an even greater distain for the entire judicial system.

Wait, it gets worse. During a break, we are standing in the hallway in a remote corner out of sight. We can see, however, the defendant who was just being cross-examined standing by a window in a secluded section of the hallway when around the corner comes the female prosecuting attorney to meet up with him. To our amazement, they begin to kiss and hug; what the hell is this, she is the one trying to convict this guy.

When court resumes, it is late in the afternoon and it appears the judge wants to wrap up for the day, and since it is a Friday, they will not reconvene until a later date.

But before the trial ends, there comes a note from the jury through the bailiff with a request from one of the members. The request is that she be released from being sequestered for the weekend, so she can attend the wedding of her daughter in Las Vegas.

The judge replies that he will take it under advisement and to wait in the court room, but before the judge can leave the bench, a remark from one of the defendants blurts out, "Oh, yeah, your honor, we are planning on going to that wedding, too." There is no reply from the judge, just a stern glance toward the defense attorney, and off he goes to chambers. My attorney and I leave without waiting for the reply. I can't help but think what a sham this entire system seems to be.

Our next scheduled appearance in court is a few weeks later. My attorney and I again meet for coffee prior to the Federal Court House being opened to the public. We finish our coffee chat and head over to get in line for admittance to the Court House. There are approximately forty people ahead of us as the security guards open the main doors leading toward the screening area and metal detectors.

By now I know most of the security guards by name and they know me as well. We usually greet each other by name on the days I have court, and today is no exception.

As it becomes my turn, the one guard tells me to hand him my coffee cup before going through the scanner. He hands it back to me on the other side. I notice there are plenty of others holding coffee cups while waiting for the elevator doors to open.

As a side note, this is a time when there have been several incidents where judges were injured by mailbox bombs at their homes, so I now had a question for the guards.

I ask, "Do you usually have people going through the scanner hand you their coffee cups rather than put them through the scanner?"

"Yes," they reply, "we don't want to have anything spill on the belt."

"Well," I say, "how do you know someone hasn't wrapped any kind of explosive or a small pistol and put it in a large coffee cup to get past the metal detectors?"

There is a long blank stare on their faces and quickly they direct everyone who has already gone through the scanner to go back on the other side, and if they have any coffee or beverage cups, to dispose of them in the trash contained before they enter the metal detector.

I get a smirk of a look from the guards as they shake their heads and say, "Thanks, Bob," but I know in their head they are thinking, what a dangerous mistake that could have been if something bad had happened.

At this juncture, the judge is becoming frustrated with this whole trial and calls a management conference to find a way to wrap this up. It's decided that at the next appearance, he will find against me in his order on finding of facts and not conclusions of law. The difference is finding of facts cannot be appealed, but the order continues to allow for my filing a claim for compensation with the US Claims Court, which we did but with no relief.

I had enough of this bullshit. Time to cut my loses and move on but now with a total disrespect for the law and all connected with it.

It proved to be a time when I should have put my ego aside and listened to my wife, but growing up around the guys I did, surrender was never an option. Through all of this, my family, especially my wife, stood by me and never said, "I told you so."

My dad, whose respect and approval I sought and took years to earn, was now in jeopardy. He watched me grow from a street kid to a college grad to a family man with a successful business. He was proud but disliked my attitude. He was not aware of all that was going on in my life and my methods were not his style.

He stood by me through those tough days, although once in a while, I could see the sadness in his eyes. I guess he thought after all those years, I would have finally learned who he really was and would learn from what he had accomplished. Once in a while I would reflect on something my grandfather told me.

"God put his son Jesus on this earth to show us the way, he walked the earth for thirty-three years, and after that time, they crucified and killed him, the next day the sun still came up! You're not that important"

After four years and 1.5 million dollars later fighting the government, I was back where I started. Bruised but not beaten. I learned from the experience and survived to fight another day. That day is just now revealing itself and with a little luck, the results may prove to be better.

My dad at desk

40th birthday party at Diamond Beach, New Jersey with brother Bill

In front of Boston Oyster House with Ben Franklin

CHAPTER SIXTEEN
New Page In My Life's Book

I was beginning to shed the cloak of arrogance and vale of indifference to find I could exist in a world of tolerance and compassion, if I would just open my eyes and mind to new possibilities. This was a foreign concept to me, but I will keep an open mind to change.

My sons were involved in sports and Scouting and I made a commitment to share in their experiences. It was a joy to be with them, for I saw promise and hope in their eyes every day. My relationship with my wife was less tumultuous, peace and calm were finding their way back into my life.

Although not conscious of what was happening at that time, but looking back on it now, I realize I made some good choices in life and seemed to be heading in the right direction once again.

But on occasion, when alone and in quiet, I close my eyes as if in a trance and can see that little boy, walking around his childhood neighborhood with a slightly tattered wool coat and cap, carrying his shoeshine box while snow swirls around him. With a determined look on his face, heading to the corner of his street to the pool hall, where the events that would shape his young life will begin to wash over him, and find myself softly mumbling to myself, "Turn around, don't go inside, it's not too late," knowing in reality, it was too late. All I can do now is accept what my life was and try to put up a warning sign for others, even if I can stop one little boy from opening up the door to his pool room.

Trying is hard, now and again falling into the same old habits of my past. Again and again, I would pick myself up and keep moving forward. My family was my inspiration, and I keep a close relationship with them, especially my sons. I didn't want them to fall into the same traps I did and encouraged them to choose a career path not riddled with temptation. My heart is full of pride, both have achieved the rank of Eagle Scout and both have attained college degrees, one chose law and the other engineering.

I couldn't help but feel that God had not abandoned me but was watching over my life and my family. No longer feeling everything was under my control; the more I opened up my eyes to possibilities, the more positive events entered my life.

I had spent the last five years restructuring my business and personal life. There was a sense of happiness, and we are looking toward a future bright with promise and growth. We were making plans on how to enjoy life, uncluttered by obligation and necessity. Our sons were on their own paths becoming young men with lives to live and enjoy.

It was not to be…the economy was beginning to turn and it did not look pretty. I began to set a strategy to protect what I had achieved in order to keep my family safe and fiscally secure.

I found there were many negative and destructive forces at work against me. So now not only did I have to solve new problems on a daily basis but had to seek out and destroy my enemies. Recognizing the emotions welling up inside and knew how dangerous and vindictive I could be if pushed, it would become a matter of self-preservation. I have been there before. I needed to unshackle my killer instincts, vowing that anyone who had a part in planning my demise would be dealt with in the cruelest manner possible once this crisis passed, not letting on what I knew and just let them hang themselves in the process.

My personal attorney and close friend told me, *"Revenge is a dish best served up cold."* I loved it; it had an appealing ring and it was what kept me focused and determined to work my way out.

Make no mistake, these were dark and vicious times. Eventually letting go of anything you might call Christian behaviors and went full steam ahead, looking only at my desired goal. It didn't matter who got hurt, it was either them or me, and I always picked me.

There was a sense of satisfaction attacking those who took part in kicking me while I was down, especially since they never saw it coming. They had no idea that I knew.

I wanted not only a pound of flesh but the blood that would come with that. Now it was my turn, and paybacks are a bitch. I needed to destroy my enemies on all levels possible, or else the cycle could repeat itself and there would be another battle down the road.

By 1995 things were beginning to turn around and life was getting easier once again. I looked around at the carnage I had left behind and was saddened by what I saw. Telling myself I only did what had to be done but knew in my heart of hearts it could have been accomplished with less destruction and rage.

This can't be all there is to life, constant vigilance, always looking over your shoulder, always weary of a fight that might come, preparing for the worst, and never truly having peace of mind.

There has to be a positive force in my life. Something to focus my energy and talents on that would produce results to build upon. I was becoming more retrospective in my life and wanted a new beginning. The old life pattern would eventually kill me if I continue down that road.

CHAPTER SEVENTEEN
Reopening An Old Door

You never know when a life changing opportunity will present itself. I was still a member of the Masonic Fraternity but not active. As luck would have it, a friend of my eldest son called me and asked if I would meet with him to discuss the Freemasons.

He had been reading about the fraternity and was extremely curious. He knew I was a member and wanted some insight. Meeting with him many times over a matter of weeks discussing the teachings of the fraternity and its precepts. He asked if I would sponsor him for membership. The motto of the fraternity is "To Be One, Ask One;" you have to find a Master Mason to act as your initial sponsor, which in many cases is not easy since the fraternity has a very subtle presence. He didn't have to look far to find me! I setup a meeting for he and I to meet with several other members of my Blue Lodge. He was excited, and I was excited for him; it reminded me why I joined the fraternity in the first place and slowly, once again, I became active in my Lodge.

That one small decision would reopen my mind and heart and reminds me what impact one-man can have on others by holding himself to a higher standard, always trying to do the right thing and not necessarily the easy thing.

Once again drawn into my Lodge and nurtured by many of my Masonic Brethren. Their encouragement and support caused me to move ahead in the Lodge's business, which was both demanding and rewarding. I began to grow in a number of ways, but most importantly it was spiritually uplifting.

I was elected to Junior Warden, the following year elected to Senior Warden, and finally the following year, elected to Lodge's highest office, that of Worshipful Master. I wasn't worshiped; it is a title of respect taken from old English society.

During that time, I visited many other Lodges here and abroad. No matter where I traveled, a member of a Masonic Lodge was there to greet me, instantly befriended, and looked after. Learning many new and interesting things about the fraternity and myself along the way. Because of my station within the Fraternity, I was respected and even admired by some. That comes with a great deal of responsibility.

Meeting with many groups and giving numerous talks on the ideals of the Masonic Fraternity was inspirational. It allowed me to communicate with many men who wanted something more meaningful in their lives, and in turn many men were drawn to me. That kind of notoriety required a cautious and tempered response to questions from those who put value and weight on your responses.

Being well-known in the Philadelphia area, I found new purpose and direction for who I had become and what I represented. The Grand Lodge of Pennsylvania called upon me for help, and I was appointed to the high office of District Deputy Grand Master for Masonic District "A." Seven Masonic Lodges were put under my authority consisting of over 3,000 members. All matters of a Masonic nature are to be directed to the District Deputy for council and resolution, his decision and determinations are autonomous. One acts carefully when given that kind of authority. It causes you to act and react more cautiously, employing fairness, justice, and equity in everything. Those demands made me a better person, more reflective, and even more spiritual. Members approach you with all types of issues and concerns, and although my obligation was limited to Masonic issues, my affection for my Brethren pushes me to do whatever I could to help. It might be Masonic, but it could be marital, medical, financial, religious, or family related. My opinion on virtually anything had meaning to them, and that weight becomes heavy. It is almost as if I were their confessor.

There are two sides to this fraternity, the altruistic side, which people do not understand. They wonder how such a characteristic could even exist in the society we now find ourselves, but nevertheless, it is there.

I must admit it is harder to live up to the high standards and teachings of Freemasonry, but you have a point of reference a benchmark so to speak, from which you can gauge your life. This aspect has always been the draw for me; it is why most men join to begin with. They want to be part of something bigger than themselves.

And bigger it is, much more so than meets the eye. There is a sinister side to all of this as well, sinister because of misconception and perception, not necessarily out of reality. I have been a member for a long time and have risen through the ranks from the bottom to the top. I know power exists there, how much influence can be brought to bear. Speaking for myself, I used my affiliation in many situations. In the way I presented myself in public, my street persona and my knowledge of the history allowed me to be a beacon for others to approach and question. In most cases, it was out of the want for knowledge and enlightenment, but there were always those lurking in the shadows just outside my focus, listening, trying not to be obvious but never successful in the task.

They are curious but nervous, intrigued but scared. I could always see in their faces that cautious look. Does this well-groomed man in the black tuxedo present a possible danger, there is a fear of getting too close.

Would I steal their soul, take over their mind, or mark them somehow for the later identification of an evil spirit? The Masons, some believe, have the power to rule the world and control everything that happens in it, they believe that the inner circle of the fraternity, of which I was a part, derived its power in influence through demonic rituals.

Admittedly the Freemasons both enjoy and suffer from the opinions of the outside world. Most of which have been born out of ignorance and jealousy. Some conceptions have a basis but can't be fully understood unless you have crossed the threshold to true Masonic light and knowledge and therefore left to draw a conclusion from their unverified assumptions. It is an old and mysterious organization with many rituals and ceremonies, which take place behind guarded and locked doors; that fact alone subjects the organization to the conspiracy theorists. There is a lot to know and even more to find out.

I have served my prescribed time as District Deputy, which lasted over five years, my commitment to my Fraternity and those Brethren with whom I have forged a permanent bond remains intact. You never stop being a Freemason, the ideals with which you lived your life are not diminished with time, you don't stop trying to do the right thing, for that would make your entire life a farce and reduce your character to that of being a pawn in the chess game of life.

But now here I stand, firm in my convictions yet receptive to ideas and opinions of others. I am secure in my beliefs and once again keenly aware of my spiritual side. I am on my journey toward that place from which no traveler returns. I will be ready, I will gladly share the light with others, and when my time finally arrives, I will close my eyes with the peace in knowing I have done my best and surrender my soul to my creator, the Great Architect of The Universe, in confidence.

For the clock of life is wound but once, my clock still ticks with the hope that I can, with each new day, look in the mirror and like who I see. My trespasses have been many but my amends were as well.

Masonic Temple of The Grand Lodge of Pennsylvania, Philadelphia

Philadelphia Masonic Temple, Egyptian Hall
My Lodge Room as Master of Equity Lodge

Corinthian Hall, Grand Lodge Meeting Hall for me as District Deputy

As Master of Equity Lodge with District Deputy Thomas Miller District "A"

**Formal Installation as District Deputy Grand Master, Masonic District "A",
January 10, 2004 Front Row, far left**

January 10, 2004 with Right Worshipful Grand Master, William Slater

CHAPTER EIGHTEEN
Conclusion

At the outset of this book, I admitted that I had no idea where my writing would lead or what revelations I might encounter along the way.

It is difficult not to glaze over the events in your life to make it as palatable as we might like in order to maintain a positive self-image. I tried not to glamorize my life or later the facts as they took place but to recall the events as accurately as I could, knowing I would experience a level of remorse that must be dealt with and resolved. To do otherwise would generate a fiction and not an honest reflection of a life lived, incorporating both the positive and negative aspects. By actually writing down and reading the occurrences, some of which I have repressed for years, I am now able to find closure and peace.

Everything in life happens for a reason. I was destined to make the choices I did and endure the experiences generated by those choices. But life and our contact with others is equivalent to a game of dominos. Once the first piece is pushed, there is no control over which piece will fall next in line or direction the subsequent pieces will fall. Any alteration to that process would undoubtedly produce a different outcome and change the place where I am now. Think about it, if you do not like where you are and would gladly accept a do over, think again. The slightest change in our past will surely change your life and your future.

Our Creator has given us free will, but our destiny is predetermined. All we can change is how we get there and how much good or evil we have expelled along the way.

We can, and I now will, have a heightened sense of my voluntary actions. I still expect to fail time and again but hope to make better decisions.

Temptations are a gift from God. What I mean by that is by experiencing a temptation, we build up spiritual antibodies to help fight off the larger and more destructive temptations that will inevitably confront us in life.

There are many issues I am currently dealing with which must be resolved, mostly of a business nature but stressful nonetheless. With my renewed connection with my inner self. I can now find peace and strength to get through the adversities.

But there are places within me I know are dark and vengeful. I keep the doors to those places locked and under guard. I have learned what I am capable of when threatened. I have always struggled with the axiom of turning the other cheek. I am not that guy! My body language sends out a strong signal to others, which says *do not provoke, the danger within is larger than it may appear.*

I can still recall, as though it were yesterday, my angler in the shadows, guys like Jimmy from the pool hall, standing off to the side just enough to seem harmless. In their mind, they thought they were harmless, dangling the bait of easy money for small favors, waiting for a nibble. I took that bait, and once hooked by the angler, he led me through creeks, ponds, streams, and eventually into the open sea, there to sink or swim. Swim to the boat of an even more skillful angler casting a bigger piece of bait, waiting for an even bigger fish.

I was lucky, my story did not end in tragedy. Well, at least not my tragedy. Considering the events in my life that could have just as easily gone wrong. I have to believe in a bigger power, something watching out for me, pushing me in the right direction, or was it just luck?

I've seen the business side of that kind of life and I've seen some of the worst. The sight of a man lying on a sofa in a back office with a .22 caliber pistol in his hand and a hole in his temple because he couldn't repay a debt or a well-dressed street associate laying in a gutter next to the open door of his Cadillac because he was next in line to the Don and the underboss blown up as he opens the front door to his home, and finally the sight of the family boss betrayed by his own associates and having the back of his head shattered by a shotgun blast through his car window. That is the life they choose, it is far different than the movies and television versions, which tend to glamorize that life. They haven't seen it up close and personal.

Looking back I am amazed by and was unaware of my ability to walk a very fine line. Things could have gone either way, my life now could have been very different. Even now as I struggle to work my way back to a good place, I must remain vigilant. It would be easy to call on my past experiences and "release the Kraken." I sometimes look at my past as an addiction, just like alcohol, drugs, or even cigarettes, it only takes one slip up to fall back on old habits.

For now I have comfort in knowing my guardian is always at my side, and when called upon, he always answers. I never feel alone and enjoy the company of a companion who never lets you down. It is your spirit guide, your conscience.

From my own experience, I caution the reader to be honest with yourself and follow your heart; it will surely lead you to the right decision. Keeping this in mind, I can tell you it is never too late to turn your life around. In the end, good will always prevail because your judgment day will be conducted by your creator, and the witness to your actions will be your own conscience.

With the help of family and friends, I hope to maintain the direction I have outlined here. Only time will tell how successful I will be or how many times I may fail. As for your children, it's your responsibility to warn them life is not always fair and you will not always be there to save them.

Give them the gift of street smarts, knowledge, and fear. They can follow their instincts if they have the tools. You cannot shelter them from harm, you can only teach them how to survive, even if it means harsh choices. There are no second chances in life if you get it wrong the first time.

What will they do, when out of the corner of their eye they see a harmless-looking man with a crooked smile, standing in the shadows holding a pole with tempting bait on the line, for even if they can't reach up to grab it, he will gladly lower the pole and bait to meet their waiting hand.

For he is the one, the timeless and ageless angler, **THE ANGLER IN THE SHADOWS!**